DAY TRIP DISCOVERIES

Selected New Mexico Excursions

Published by

NEW MEXICO MAGAZINE

Mak Nohl

First paperback edition 1993
by *New Mexico Magazine*

Copyright © by *New Mexico Magazine*

ISBN 0-937206-26-1

Library of Congress Catalog
Card Number 92-064108

New Mexico Magazine
495 Old Santa Fe Trail
Santa Fe, New Mexico 87503

***Front and back cover**—One of many
natural cisterns near Ácoma Pueblo
collects water from rain and snowfall
year-round, while pueblo residents keep
the area around the watering hole swept
and clean to ensure good water. San
Estévan del Rey Mission dominates the
pueblo area while Mount Taylor is visible
on the far left of the back cover. Photo by
Mark Nohl.*

DAY TRIP DISCOVERIES

Edited by
Arnold Vigil

Designed and produced by
Richard C. Sandoval

Typesetting by
Linda J. Vigil

C O N T E N T S

PREFACE

The expansive New Mexico landscape offers almost limitless possibilities for travel, exploration and adventure. Cultural and historical points of interest throughout the state also provide a long list of destinations for motivated and interested travelers.

As any aficionado of New Mexico knows, narrowing down specific points of interest to visit in this vast state can be a very perplexing decision, especially when limited time is a factor. Fortunately, New Mexico offers plenty of sites that can be adequately absorbed in one day as well as places well-suited for extended stays.

In the late 1980s *New Mexico Magazine* instituted the monthly column "All in a Day," which offers concise information about single-day excursions to popular and not-so-well-known destinations within the state.

Because of the large number of potential destinations this state has to offer, deciding upon one particular site for a day trip story presents quite a dilemma for the editors of *New Mexico Magazine* every month.

DAY TRIP DISCOVERIES: Selected New Mexico Excursions represents more than four years' accumulation of "All in a Day" stories written by 36 knowledgeable writers statewide. Each story is categorized into one of six statewide regions for easy reference and accessibility from virtually any community in New Mexico. The magazine uses the same regional breakdown in its "Sundial" calendar each month.

When applicable, each story contains historical, cultural and geographical information that gives the visitor an excellent background understanding of a particular site. This comes in especially handy when visiting the more rural destinations.

Telephone numbers for specific sites, if available, are listed in each story. We urge visitors to call ahead because some sites, or the roads leading to them, might be closed due to inclement weather or seasonal circumstances.

The latest information concerning road conditions is available by calling the state Highway and Transportation Department's toll-free hotline at (800) 432-4269.

Regional breakdowns include the northwest, north-central, northeast, southeast, southwest and central portions of the state. Each geographical section has its own distinct character with unique attributes that set it apart from the rest of the state.

The northwest section of the state includes San Juan, McKinley and Cíbola counties and the principal cities of Farmington, Bloomfield, Gallup and Grants. Much of this section is dominated by the Navajo, Zuñi, Ácoma and Laguna Indian reservations.

The rolling, multicolored hills and mountains of the northwest are a sightseer's paradise as is 11,301-foot Mount Taylor near Ácoma Pueblo. Besides the specific sites listed in this book, the northwest offers dozens of other ancient destinations that tantalize the imagination.

Many of the state's most dramatic mountain areas sit within the

more on page 8

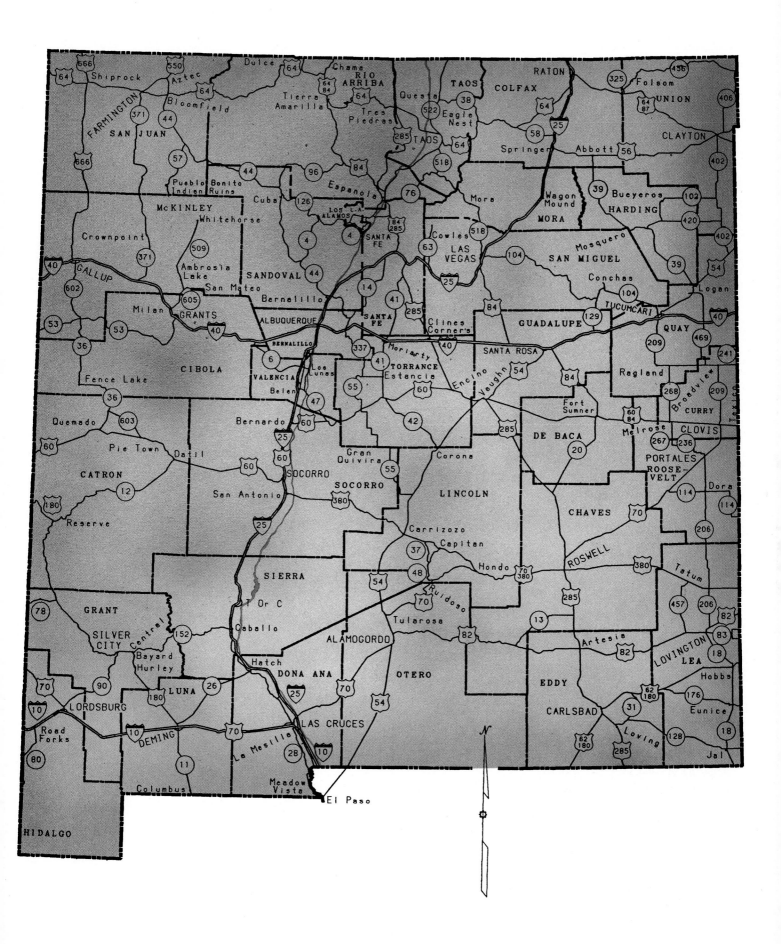

continued from page 6

north-central section, which includes Río Arriba, Taos, Los Alamos, Santa Fe and most of Sandoval counties, plus the Sangre de Cristo and Jémez mountain ranges.

Most of the northern Indian pueblos are located within the north-central region as well as the Jicarilla Apache Indian Reservation. The principal cities include Taos, Española, Santa Fe, Chama and Los Alamos, birthplace of the world's first atomic bomb.

The plains of northeastern New Mexico differ dramatically from the terrain of the northwest and north-central regions. It is here that the Great Plains of the central United States meet the eastern flank of the southern Rocky Mountains, creating a plethora of natural phenomena.

The northeast includes the counties of Colfax, Union, Mora, Harding, San Miguel, Quay and Guadalupe and the principal cities of Ratón, Tucumcari, Las Vegas, Angel Fire and Las Vegas.

The rolling green plains of the north give way to the semiarid, desertlike conditions of the southeast, with the larger cities of Clovis, Portales, Hobbs, Roswell, Carlsbad, Artesia, Alamogordo and Ruidoso.

Including the counties of De Baca, Curry, Roosevelt, Lincoln, Chaves, Lea, Eddy and Otero, the southeast region also is home to the Mescalero Apache Indian Reservation, the Sacramento and Guadalupe mountains plus the Capitán range, once the romping grounds of Billy the Kid and birthplace and gravesite of Smokey Bear, a national fire-prevention institution.

The southwestern section of the state contains the first officially designated wilderness area in the nation—the Gila Wilderness. Many an Old West mining town sprouted, prospered and died in this region whose counties include Catron, Socorro, Sierra, Grant, Hidalgo, Luna and Doña Ana.

Among the larger cities of the southwest are Las Cruces, Deming, Silver City, Truth or Consequences and Socorro. The southwest region offers a mountainous glimpse of New Mexico's Wild West past and its developing future. It also includes lands of the Alamo Band of the Navajo Indian tribe.

New Mexico's most populated region lies in the central section, with Albuquerque, Rio Rancho and Belén taking honors as the principal cities. The Sandía and Manzano mountain ranges offer scenic backdrops throughout most of the region while the Río Grande bisects its western portion.

The central section includes Torrance, Valencia, Bernalillo and a portion of Sandoval counties along with the Indian lands of Laguna, Isleta, Sandía and San Felipe pueblos.

DAY TRIP DISCOVERIES: Selected New Mexico Excursions offers visitors many brief introductions to this diverse land of New Mexico, a state like no other in the nation. With elevations ranging from more than 13,000 feet to as low as 2,800 feet, New Mexico's diversity is unsurpassed geologically as well as culturally.

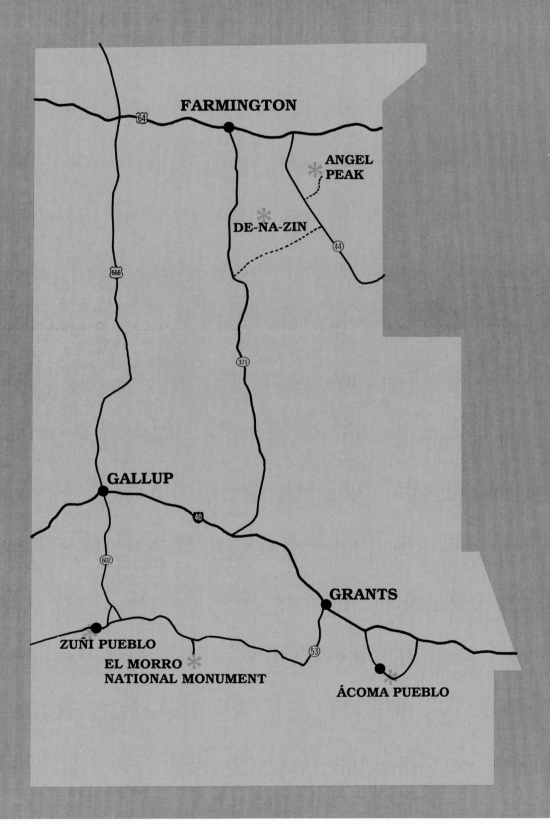

Mark Nohl

Sky City remains the focal point for feast day activities at Ácoma Pueblo.

Ácoma Pueblo

by Melanie J. Majors

Permanence—in the form of clay and rock—remains as the simple testament of an ancient city called Ácoma, the Sky City.

Three wind-carved sandstone formations, Dinosaur Rock, Lonesome Rock and Camel Rock, silently guard the entrance to the 367-foot sandstone monolith, the foundation for the oldest continuously inhabited city in the United States. Ácoma oral historians tell visitors that the mesa has been home to the Ácoma people since A.D. 600 while archaeologists confirm occupation back to A.D. 1150.

More than 2,900 people live at Ácoma, pronounced EH-ko-ma or AH-ko-ma. While the pueblo has settlements at Acomita, Anzac and McCarty's, it's Sky City, sometimes called Old Ácoma, that attracts more than 75,000 visitors annually.

The ideal defensive location, the distinctive people and the village's architecture have fascinated visitors since Francisco Vázquez de Coronado led the first white man to the site. Today's visitors still marvel at the architectural features of the Ácomas' 3-story dwellings—clay and rock homes that face south to capture the sun's warmth during winter and feature thick, blank northern walls as protection against cold winds.

About 10 families live in Sky City year-round. Maintaining their traditional ways, they heat their homes with fragrant piñon wood, have no electricity, natural gas, indoor plumbing or telephones. Most operate businesses, selling trademarked, monochrome Ácoma pottery, jewelry and food. Another 300 to 400 families occupy their ancient skyscrapers on feast days.

These festivals take place at the centrally located kiva or the San Estévan del Rey Mission. Ancient handhewn ladders ensure limited access for private rituals in the above-ground kivas.

In contrast, the massive San Estévan del Rey Mission is open to all. The mission stands as a serene monument to those Ácomas who carried or hauled massive amounts of rock and wood up the mesa's steep slopes.

Built over a 10-year period beginning in 1629, the mission grew to occupy a 70-acre site on the mesa. Religious artwork from Spain adorns the adobe structure, which features a packed dirt floor, 18th-century wood carvings, an outdoor classroom and rooms for the clergy.

Just outside the church's main entrance lies the pueblo's cemetery. It, too, represents a tremen-

dous effort from the Ácomas—tons of sand for the burial ground were brought up the mesa on the backs of the residents. These master builders even included an adobe wall topped with mute clay sentries to keep intruders out of the cemetery.

Until the mid-1950s access to the quiet mesa was limited to a steep stone staircase on the west side called Padre's Trail. Today a gravel road allows vehicles to reach Sky City.

"At Ácoma you see that a part of the past is still very real today," says Mary Tenorio, a tourist center manager.

To reach Ácoma from Albuquerque, drive west on Interstate 40 approximately 50 miles. Take Exit 108 and drive 12 miles to the Ácoma Visitor Center. Traveling east from Gallup, drive about 90 miles on I-40, take Exit 102 and travel 11

Above—A dirt road leading up to Old Ácoma skirts by a row of corrals fashioned from indigenous materials. The name Ácoma is from the Keres Indian language—ako, meaning "white rock" and ma, "people," together "people of the white rock."

miles to the center.

All visitors must register at the center. Admission is free to the museum, which houses a permanent exhibit, Ácoma pottery, the canes of authority and other artifacts belonging to the pueblo. Food, drinks and crafts may be purchased and shaded picnic tables are provided.

The pueblo offers daily Sky City guided tours, full of insight and centuries-old legends. Unaccompanied visitors are not allowed. Sturdy shoes, sunscreen and a hat are a must for the one-hour walking tour. Following the tour, visitors may descend the stone staircase of Padre's Trail or return to the center by bus.

Tour fees are charged for adults, seniors, children and picture-taking. The cemetery and the mission interior are off limits. Pets are not permitted on the tours, but can be left in kennels at the visitor center on a space-available basis.

In addition to the daily tours, visitors may attend several of the feast days during the year. Call first, since some celebrations are closed to the public. Backpacking, camping or hiking on rock formations, including 400-foot-high Enchanted Mesa, just a few miles east of Ácoma, are prohibited. ⚜

Above—*Remnants of Spanish influence are quite evident in the church at Ácoma, San Estévan del Rey, built over a 10-year period starting in 1629. The Pueblo village was first reported by the Spanish in 1540 by Hernando de Alvarado, one of Francisco Vázquez de Coronado's men.*

Mark Nohl

Millions of years of ice and wind have carved the jagged hills of the Nacimiento badlands.

Angel Peak

Beyond the stark desert to the north, the stunning peaks of the San Juan Mountains and La Plata scrape the clouds.

by Electa Draper

Large fallen boulders collect in the gentle folds of the Nacimiento badlands. Soft grays, powdery greens, warm golds and muted lavenders streak the wrinkled and parched earth. Stunted juniper and cedar trees crouch on disintegrating ledges.

This mysterious, extraterrestrial landscape can be explored by taking a six-mile detour off of N.M. 44, down a good dirt road southwest of Farmington in northwestern New Mexico, to the rim of the Angel Peak Recreation Area. Here, visitors can pull into the Sage picnic site, the Cliff View or Angel Peak Overlook.

The incongruity of friendly and mundane picnic tables, benches and awnings perched near the awesome desolation of the badlands of Angel Peak jars the senses. But it offers the perfect opportunity to snack on sandwiches and sip sodas while scanning the landscape shaped through millions of years by wind and ice. A crumbling stone figure, interpreted in past ages as Twin Angels, Lost Angels or Angel Peak, dominates the view. Its immense sandstone blocks stand ready to drop into another page of history.

Visitors can see 360 degrees of confusingly varied terrain. Beyond the stark desert to the north, the stunning peaks of the San Juan Mountains and La Plata scrape the clouds. To the west loom the mysterious form of Shiprock and the barely discernible outline of the Lukachukai Mountains in Arizona. To the south, across a restful green sea of sage flecked with purple larkspur and red Indian paintbrush, is the mesa of the Navajo Origin Myth, El Huérfano (the orphan). Easy trails for foot or bicycle radiate in all directions.

Forty million years ago, in the Tertiary Age, an inland sea covered the badlands. When the waters receded, they left behind layers upon crushing layers of mud and sand that metamorphosed into shale and sandstone. Vulnerable to the violence of frost and streams of air, these sediments were contorted into the ragged Nacimiento and San José formations. The San José formation was the hard cap over the softer layers of sandstone. The remnants of this rocky strata are the 100 feet known as Angel Peak. Though towering only those 100 feet, its shape is imposing enough to be called a peak.

The area is rich in oil and gas. Wells and roads crisscross the country. In the depths of Kutz Canyon, just below the picnic facilities, lurk other ancient souvenirs of the ancient sea. Fossils of mammals, dinosaurs, reptiles and plants are continuously exhumed by erosion.

No artifacts of human habitation exist. There never was enough water at Angel Peak for prehistoric man. Early man knew of it, however. Indians called the place *Tsethl Gizhi*, "rock on top of two prongs." Navajos refer to it as the dwelling place of the Sacred Ones. The Spaniards named it Nacimiento, "the birthplace."

The road system built by the Indians of the Chaco Canyon settlements only skirted the edges of the badlands. It was a thousand years later before the first permanent human features appeared—structures for extracting oil and gas and the picnic shelters for those who come to drink in the solitude and haunting beauty.

Rock hunting is permitted on federal lands that include more than 10,000 acres. Land-status maps are available from the Bureau of Land Management to help the rock hound or wanderer distinguish between private and public roads and lands.

The badlands and Angel Peak are located 35 miles south of Farmington off of N.M. 44. Indian trading posts at Blanco and Nageezi are south of the Angel Peak turnoff.

For more information write to the Bureau of Land Management, Farmington Resource Area, 1235 La Plata Highway, Farmington, NM 87401 or call (505) 327-5300.

The barren but beautiful hills of Angel Peak Recreation Area support nothing but the hardiest of life-forms. Once covered by an inland sea some 40 million years ago, the area often reveals evidence of ancient animals and plants.

Mark Nohl

Badlands and massive petrified logs color this wilderness area in northwestern New Mexico.

De-na-zin

Fossilized dinosaurs, plants, mammals and reptiles also can be found in De-na-zin.

by Ed Tisdale

Navajo legend holds that flocks of migratory cranes stopped to wash and rest at De-na-zin in the state's northwestern corner on their way south for the winter.

In Navajo, *de-na-zin* means the standing crane. A pictograph painted on a sandstone wall near this Bureau of Land Management wilderness area depicts the bird.

De-na-zin is relatively new as a wilderness area. Although designated a national wilderness by Congress in 1984, De-na-zin's 22,454 acres in San Juan County are prehistoric in form and character.

What millions of years ago was a swamp, complete with dinosaurs, is now a colorful but barren landscape of mesas and badlands seemingly incapable of supporting any but the hardiest life.

But piñon, juniper, yucca, cactus and other vegetation can be found flourishing in the arid sands and shale hills. Animal life includes scattered doves, quail, coyotes, hawks, lizards and snakes.

What a visitor likely won't see is another visitor, because De-na-zin offers solitude in abundance.

According to BLM estimates, fewer than 500 people a year visit the area. The small gravel parking lot doesn't get enough traffic to stem the growth of hardy weeds springing up through the spaces.

The landscape is impressive if only for its silence. A visitor can be alone with only the sound of the breeze blowing his shirt, the overhead cry of a prairie falcon or the caw of a raven swooping down from the heavens.

One unique portion of De-na-zin is called the Logjam. The approxi-

mately 350-acre section contains massive petrified logs, some attaining lengths of more than 75 feet and exceeding a diameter of 6 feet.

Red- and orange-grained petrified logs, spotted with lichen and complete with what appear to be wormholes, bark and roots, stick out from the cliff's side like ancient cannons guarding the approach to De-na-zin Wash.

Another one of De-na-zin's improbable features is a small stand of a dozen ponderosa pines huddled in the high desert. The trees are remnants of a cooler, moister time that no longer remains. Now they lie far from their usual mountainside home. The trees contain nesting grounds for hawks, falcons and golden eagles.

Elsewhere, gray corrugated fins of sandstone rise from a small canyon floor, creating an impenetrable rock-sided maze.

During a snowmelt or after a rare desert rainstorm, short-lived waterfalls dive from the canyon walls in silty flows.

Fossilized dinosaurs, plants, mammals and reptiles also can be found in De-na-zin. But taking home fossils and bits of petrified wood is discouraged.

While De-na-zin is located near Chaco Canyon and other prehistoric Indian sites, the ancient Anasazi seldom made De-na-zin their home. While some ruins exist here, they are scarce compared to the rest of the artifact-dense Four Corners region. That factor has helped keep De-na-zin relatively untouched and helped in its designation as a wilderness area.

Because the wilderness area is so remote, visitors are cautioned to be prepared. No one will be there for a rescue. Elevations average about 8,500 feet.

Above—A visit to De-na-zin can be compared with a journey to another planet without all the red tape at NASA. The area never ceases to amaze visitors with its fantastical shapes and formations.

Mark Nohl

Vehicles should be filled with fuel before the trip. Full canteens and water bottles also should be on hand. There is no reliable source of water for miles. Boots, sunglasses and a hat also are advised. Campers should know that firewood is not abundant, so cooking materials and fuel should be brought along.

To find De-na-zin drive 68 miles north of Cuba on N.M. 44, then turn west on the dirt County Road 7500 and drive 12 miles. A small wooden sign and parking area identify the entrance and border.

After crossing over into the wilderness, visitors are on their own. There are no marked trails or camping areas. Ranger visits are infrequent.

Maps, pamphlets and information about De-na-zin are available from the BLM's northwestern office, 1235 La Plata Highway, Far-

mington, N.M., (505) 327-5300. No fee or permit is required to enter.

Topographic maps and a visit to the BLM office are helpful if you are looking for specifics like the Logjam, but not necessary for a romp through the badlands, bird-watching or enjoyment of the twisting colors of the desert sunset. ⚜

Above—The arid slopes of De-na-zin once served as home to dinosaurs and other swamp creatures, whose fossils still litter the area. The solitude at the site can be quite the contrast to an urban setting.

Mark Nohl

El Morro has loomed on the horizon as a landmark and stopping place for centuries.

El Morro National Monument

by Stephen Siegfried

Could these hills but speak, what would they say? Travelers new to the country have looked out across the land and wished it could tell of those who have come before. They might as well try talking to the wind.

But in the dry, hard land of western New Mexico there is such a place, a sandstone bluff with tales to tell, a rock that records a history of the Southwest through parts of seven centuries and beyond. El Morro, Spanish for the bluff or headland, rises 200 feet above the upper Sonoran plane, 43 miles southwest of Grants on N.M. 53. A landmark for parched travelers because of a natural basin at its base, Inscription Rock tells a story of the Old West through thousands of carvings in the soft sandstone of the bluff, a massive tablet that makes known the passing of ancient civilizations, conquistadores and others who came to the oasis beside the great rock.

The trail beginning at the visitor center leads along the northern face of the bluff, en route to a deep pool that holds water throughout the year. Names, dates and messages in English and Spanish are all along the trail, but the earliest inscriptions are pre-Columbian petroglyphs that date from the 1300s. The last were made before Dec. 8, 1906, when El Morro became a national monument.

If you look closely at the cliff above the pool, you may see hand- and toeholds leading to the top of the bluff and an Anasazi village the neighboring Zuñis called *Atsinna*, or where pictures are on the rock. No one makes use of the hand- and toeholds anymore. The trail leads over the rimrock to the remnants of two pueblos, a continuing mystery for archaeologists

19

Above—Stone ruins of Anasazi dwellings sit atop a cliff at El Morro National Monument, where many historical travelers left their mark. The Zuñi Indians called the ancient community Atsinna, or "where pictures are on the rock."

to ponder.

If you close your eyes and imagine, you might hear the clatter of horse and armor, the voices of conquistadores. Not far from the pool is the inscription of Juan de Oñate, the first governor of New Spain. Oñate was coming back "from discovery of the Sea of the South, on the 16th of April, 1605," when, begins the oldest decipherable message, he *"paso por aquí."* After Oñate, many others would "pass by here" to drink from the pool and carve their names in the autograph album of Inscription Rock.

For some, the headland serves as headstone, the messages and names in the rock as epitaph. After early conquistadores and explorers gave up searching for the Seven Cities of Cíbola, the sepulcher replaced the sword as priests came to the neighboring pueblos to convert the Zuñis and Hopis to Ca-

tholicism. One message tells of travelers who stopped at El Morro on "August 5, 1629, that one may well to Zuñi pass and carry the faith." Evidently, the Zuñis didn't share in the friars' zeal—they killed and scalped the priest, Padre Letrado. An expedition to punish the Zuñis was dispatched from Santa Fe, leaving the following inscription: "They passed on the 23rd day of March, 1632, to the avenging of the death of the Father Letrado-Lujan."

The reconquest of the region after the Pueblo Revolt is documented with the message, "Here was the General Don Diego de Vargas, who conquered for our Holy Faith, and the Royal Crown all New Mexico at his own expense, the year 1692." English inscriptions begin soon after the arrival of Gen. Stephen W. Kearny in Santa Fe—the first by "Lt. J. H.

Mark Nohl

Mark Nohl

Simpson and R. H. Kern, Artist, [who] visited and copied these inscriptions, September 17th 18th 1849." Inscription Rock records the coming of the railroad in the 1870s, and with it, a change in the main east/west route. For the iron horse, a gradual grade, not the availability of water, was the limiting element of travel. El Morro was no longer an essential stop on the journey west.

The monument is open daily except Christmas. The hours are extended from Memorial Day through Labor Day. The trail from the visitor center, past the pool and over the mesatop and back, is more than two miles, but allow yourself enough time for the inscriptions and ruins. There is a shorter half-mile loop to the pool and back. The altitude is 7,200 feet, so don't rush.

The inscriptions at El Morro, like the soft sandstone of the bluff, aren't permanent. The names of some who shaped the history of the Southwest have been lost from the rock, among them, Kit Carson, whose name was mistakenly erased along with some graffiti. The forces of nature—wind, rain, and sun—will gradually dissolve those messages that speak through centuries in a brevity and precision that must come when letters and symbols are slowly, painstakingly, carved in a rock. Such messages are worth seeing. *Pase por aquí.* The rock has much to say. ✺

Above left—New Mexico's first colonizer Don Juan de Oñate left this message on Inscription Rock: "Adelantado [governor] Don Juan de Oñate passed this way from the discovery of the South Sea, April 16, 1606 [1605]." *Right*—This small watering hole must have seemed an oasis to early travelers of the semiarid terrain.

Mark Nohl

The morning's first sun rays color Hawikuh Ruins near Zuñi Pueblo.

Zuñi Pueblo

The tribe's annual round of rites, prayers and dances is designed to sustain the cycle of life. . . .

by William Clark

Zuñi Pueblo crowns a low hill above the Zuñi River in northwestern New Mexico, where rust-colored mesas banded with pink and buff-yellow sweep away toward the Arizona line.

This old village of terraced adobe and cut red-stone buildings, surrounded by outlying settlements, is New Mexico's largest Indian pueblo with a population of nearly 9,000. It's the only one with its own public school district, even its own radio station. N.M. 53 bisects the Zuñi reservation and runs through the heart of town, past the tribal offices and shops filled with the creations of local artisans—animal fetishes carved from stone, some of them exquisite miniatures strung in bright necklaces; silver jewelry bearing inlays or mosaics of turquoise, shell and jet; and needlepoint work, fine strips of sky-blue stone set in rows or sun-burst patterns, for which this pueblo is renowned.

Such arts represent the flowering of old rhythms of living that survive here with a resonance evoked in ways as simple as the aroma of bread baking in the beehive-shaped ovens clustered by the river, or as complex and mysterious as the rituals that signify the rich ceremonial life of Zuñi. The tribe's annual round of rites, prayers and dances is designed to sustain the cycle of life and ultimately leads to Shalako Day in late November or early December.

This ritual marks the culmination of the Zuñi ceremonial calendar. Sometimes open to public view, it offers a night of magic, of age-old religious impulses as the giant masked figures of the Shalakos dance through the night.

These dancers are part of a cultural continuum that stretches

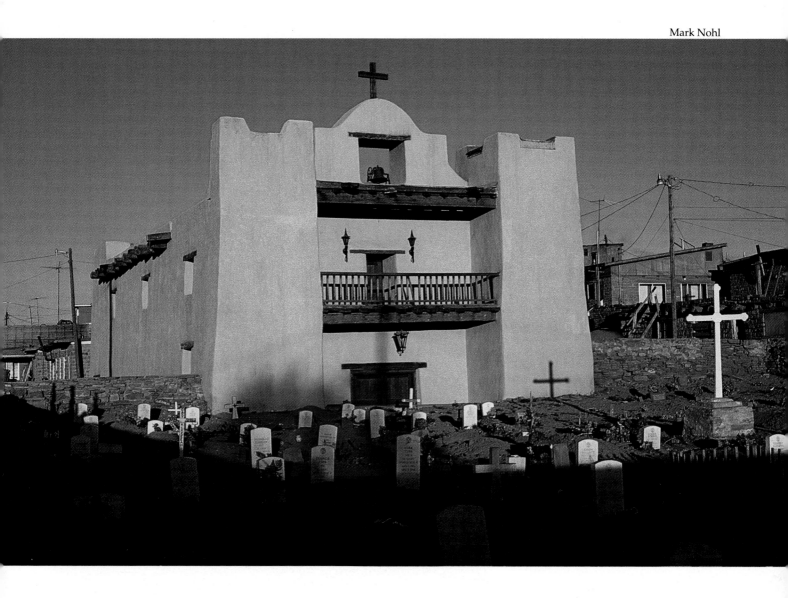

back more than 1,700 years on this reservation, an area occupied by a succession of peoples who melded influences from the prehistoric Anasazi, Mogollón and Hohokam traditions. But Zuñi looms especially large in the early recorded history of the Southwest.

Fray Marcos de Niza scouted this region for the Spanish crown in 1539, guided north by Estéban the Moor, who earlier had passed through southern New Mexico with Cabeza de Vaca's party. Estéban was killed at Zuni, but de Niza returned in 1540 with Francisco Vázquez de Coronado, seeking the Seven Cities of Cíbola—the fabled cities of gold—and his arrival at the old Zuñi village of Hawikuh marked the first contact of the indigenous people of the Southwest with an armed European expedition.

The result, unfortunately, was a battle. The Spaniards took Hawikuh by force and remained for several months before moving east into the Río Grande Valley. Coronado found no gold at Zuñi but instead discovered the cultural riches of an agricultural people skilled in arts and crafts and living in multistoried buildings of adobe and stone—a description that still fits Zuñi nicely.

The precise date of the Shalako ceremony, the high point of the Zuñi year, is set a few weeks in advance and may be learned by calling the tribal offices in November at (505) 782-4481. Accommodations are available in Gallup, 36 miles to the north via N.M. 602, and should be booked well in advance of Shalako, which draws hundreds of visitors.

The ceremony unfolds in a night of indelible, dreamlike images, as the six Shalakos, one for each of

Above—La Nuestra Señora de Guadalupe de Halona in Zuñi Pueblo was originally established by the Spanish between 1633 and 1666, but it was destroyed during the 1680 Pueblo Revolt. Later rebuilt by Franciscans, the church fell into disrepair for about a century before it was restored between 1966 and 1972.

Mark Nohl

Mark Nohl

Above—*Petroglyphs near Zuñi Pueblo reveal aspects of ancient Indian life. **Above right**—The brown pastels of a cattle watering hole and dark contours of a mesa offer a striking contrast to the azure blue New Mexico sky over Zuñi Pueblo.*

Zuñi's kivas representing the sacred directions—the heavens, earth, the four cardinal points of the compass—enter the village to visit houses specially prepared for them, which they will bless and where they will pray, feast and dance until dawn. The masks, 10-foot-tall cylindrical shapes with rounded tops, are carried on poles. They have ruffs of black plumes, round eyes, upcurved horns with a fan of eagle feathers between them and long wooden snouts split like the beaks of birds. Manipulated from inside the Shalako costume, a cone-shaped cloak of white cloth draped over hoops, the bills snap together with a sharp clapping sound.

The Shalakos occupy houses (maps indicating their locations are available when the ceremony is open to the public) decorated like works of installation art, their walls covered with Navajo weavings, brilliant flowered shawls and tapestries, stuffed animals decked with turquoise. The masked figures dance in long trenches cut in unfinished dirt floors to accommodate their great height.

The Zuñis guard the deep religious significance of this ceremony closely—no photography, sketching or sound recording is allowed. Veiled in mystery and performed in an ancient, mythic dimension of time, Shalako has the universal power of all great art. It is a night to remember.

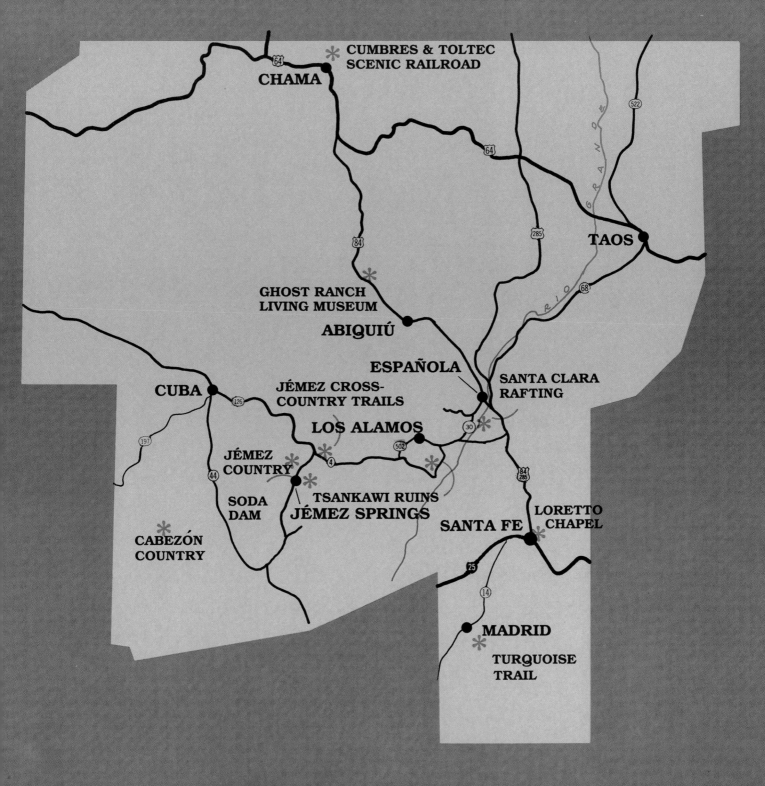

CUMBRES & TOLTEC
SCENIC RAILROAD

CHAMA

GHOST RANCH
LIVING MUSEUM

ABIQUIÚ

ESPAÑOLA

CUBA

JÉMEZ CROSS-
COUNTRY TRAILS

SANTA CLARA
RAFTING

LOS ALAMOS

TAOS

JÉMEZ
COUNTRY

TSANKAWI RUINS

SODA
DAM

JÉMEZ SPRINGS

CABEZÓN
COUNTRY

LORETTO
CHAPEL

SANTA FE

MADRID

TURQUOISE
TRAIL

Dan Scurlock

Explorers in the rugged Cabezón country might stumble upon ghost towns.

Cabezón Country

> . . . *the numerous, tower-ing volcanic peaks are excellent habitat for eagles, hawks, deer and mountain lions. A few black bears have been sighted in recent years. . . .*

by Dan Scurlock

Just before turning off N.M. 44 north of San Ysidro in Sandoval County, you get your first view of Cabezón Peak rising dramatically out of the Río Puerco Valley. As you drive west-ward toward the 2,200-foot-high volcanic plug, its dark basaltic mass appears to be the head of a mythical giant, hence its name Cabezón. The curving gravel road crosses the muddy waters of the Río Puerco on an old bridge and drops down into the land grant vil-lage of San Luís, site of the first Spanish settlement in the area, dat-ing to the 1760s.

Beyond San Luís more volcanic peaks come into view to the distant left and right of Cabezón Peak, and behind, the long, dark outline of Mesa Chivato, capped with lava flow rock from the largest volcano in the area—Mount Taylor—looms on the horizon. Paralleling the road about a mile to the right are the steep, adobe brown cliffs of San Luís Mesa.

San Luís' sister village, Cabezón, or La Posta as it was known in the late 18th century, is at the end of a side road leading south toward the Puerco at the base of Cabezón Peak. Now a virtual ghost town with only one resident family, the adobe ruins of a church, school, stage stop and three dozen or so houses are testament to ranchers and farmers who were attracted to the once fertile valley and grass-land hills. Navajo raiders, protect-ing their hunting lands and sacred shrines on Cabezón Peak, periodi-cally drove the Spaniards from the valley. Later, overgrazing, droughts and finally the Depres-sion of the 1930s forced residents to seek a livelihood in Corrales, Bernalillo or Albuquerque.

Beyond the turnoff to the village

of Cabezón the road swings south past Cerro Cuate, the Hill of the Twins, to follow the river valley. After crossing the Arroyo Chico Bridge, marked by a Bureau of Land Management sign, the road forks. The left-hand fork continues south, paralleling the river, toward the village of Guadalupe, while the other route leads up the 8,000-foot-high Mesa Chivato. Climbing the east flank of the mesa, the grasslands with scattered juniper give way to piñon and scrub oak, then ponderosa pine. Views of the valley below become increasingly riveting, especially in the changing light of late afternoon. Once again, the size and starkness of Cabezón Peak are the central focus of this truly awesome landscape.

From the mesa rim, the road leading south from Arroyo Chico is but a sinuous ribbon of caliche tan. Along the road, five miles be-low the bridge, the village of Guadalupe is hidden from view by hills. Like Cabezón, only one ranching family inhabits this nearly deserted settlement, which includes the remains of a 2-story, adobe stagecoach stop. The stage line carried mail and passengers between Santa Fe and Fort Wingate from the late-19th to the early 20th century.

Two miles beyond the village, a steep, narrow ridge juts from the edge of the road onto the flat floor of the valley. A small sign stating that the site is protected by the Federal Antiquities Act offers the only clue to the casual observer of the archaeological remains found here. A fairly steep foot trail leads from the sign up the south side of the ridge to the summit, where corrugated and black-on-white pot-sherds are strewn about the surface. Sandstone slab walls, un-

Above—*Cabezón Peak rises dramatically from the surrounding landscape during a sunset. Navajos called the volcanic plug* tse najin, *meaning "black rock."*

W.P. Fleming

earthed by University of New Mexico archaeologists in the mid-1970s, outline 25 rectangular rooms and three round kivas perched on the east end of the ridge. This small Anasazi village was part of the Chaco Canyon culture, which dominated the San Juan Basin of northwestern New Mexico in the 11th and 12th centuries.

Ridges like this one, the steep, rugged cliffs and canyons along Mesa Chivato and San Luís Mesa, and the numerous, towering volcanic peaks are excellent habitat for eagles, hawks, deer and mountain lions. A few black bears have been sighted in recent years, attesting to the rugged remoteness of the area. Because of these wildlife values, as well as for the outstanding geological, archaeological and scenic qualities of Cabezón country, the Bureau of Land Management is con-

sidering most of the area for inclusion in the National Wilderness System.

May to early June and September to October, normally periods of mild, dry weather and a profusion of wildflowers, are the best times to visit Cabezón country. To get there from Albuquerque, take Interstate 25 north to N.M. 44, driving northwest 19 miles beyond San Ysidro. Turn west on an all-weather, gravel road. Although maintained by Sandoval County, this road is not marked at the turn. As you approach the 19-mile point northwest of San Ysidro, watch for a brown sign on the right with the name Holy Ghost Recreation Area. The road to Cabezón country will be to your left, opposite the sign.

Fill your gas tank at San Ysidro and stock up on food and drink before leaving the highway—you won't find these commodities in

San Luís or points west. Nor are there marked hiking trails, picnic areas or other recreational facilities on the federal land, but these may be installed if the area is made a wilderness area. Maps, brochures and other information may be obtained from the BLM office in Albuquerque (505) 761-8700. Camp and picnic sites, drinking water and fishing are available at the Holy Ghost Recreation Area, maintained by Jémez Pueblo. ❈

Above—*The village of Cabezón was first settled in 1826 under the name La Posta by Juan Maestas who arrived from Pagosa Springs, Colo. The name was changed to Cabezón in 1891 largely due to the efforts of a man named Oliver Perry Hovey.*

Mark Nohl

Steam-powered, coal-fired locomotives generally remain relics of the past, but they are quite common in Chama on the Cumbres & Toltec Scenic Railroad.

Cumbres & Toltec Scenic Railroad

Travelers on the C&TSR are thrust into the past as the coal-powered locomotive acts as a time machine. . . .

by Arnold Vigil

As time slips into the 20th century, living relics will be harder to find because they've served out their usefulness. But they will remain as an important link to our past.

The Cumbres & Toltec Scenic Railroad, a 64-mile stretch of narrow-gauge rail more than 100 years old between Chama and Antonito, Colo., continues to survive the test of time. The railroad has shifted from a mode of necessary transportation to fulfilling the aesthetics of the historically minded.

Completed in 1880 by the Denver & Rio Grande Railway Co. as a means to transport precious ores from mines in Durango and Silverton, Colo., it's seen the coming and going of mining, oil and timbering booms, two world wars and its own near extinction. Rides on the antique railway start in late May and continue through mid-October.

Travelers on the C&TSR are thrust into the past as the coal-powered locomotive acts as a time machine, chugging visitors through steep Rocky Mountain slopes, green valleys, ancient trestles and enchanting tunnels. It skirts a side of 1,100-foot Toltec Gorge, testing the equilibrium of even the most adventurous.

In 1968, the then Denver & Rio Grande Western wanted to end the once-prosperous railroad. But a handful of concerned historians and railroad buffs saw the move as the death of living history. They convinced the states of New Mexico and Colorado to purchase the railway system for $547,000. The package came complete with 150 freight cars, nine locomotives (still in use) and 64 miles of track with eight sidings.

"That was a real undertaking—

Above—*Riders on the C&TSR often journey above the clouds, especially when going through the Toltec Gorge. Fall is an especially popular time because of the ever-changing mountain colors.*

to get two states to agree on something—much less to buy a railroad," says Jack Wiedman, a fireman and a brakeman on the C&TSR, which crosses the New Mexico/Colorado border 11 times.

Reservations must be made to ride the railroad, which transports nearly 40,000 travelers each season. Although discouraged, walk-ons can be accommodated if space permits.

Two trains start simultaneously at Chama and Antonito and they meet at Osier, Colo., roughly the midway point of the six-and-a-half hour ride. Both trains stop at Osier, where lunch is offered at a nominal cost. Otherwise, people may bring their own food. Alcohol isn't allowed on the trains, which offer snack bars and souvenirs.

Travelers can take a short trip and ride the train back to Chama after lunch at Osier. The full tour

travels on to Antonito, where vans bring travelers back to Chama in about an hour.

The full tour from Chama is recommended. The ride from Osier features a 366-foot-long tunnel through unsupported solid rock and a 349-foot-long mud tunnel braced with wood and forged through volcanic ash. Railworkers constructed both tunnels in 1879 and 1880. The narrow-gauge rails skirt one edge of the Toltec Gorge with an 1,100-foot drop.

The ride from Osier has two trestles—the Cascade Trestle is 409 feet long and 137 feet high, and the Lobato Trestle is 340 feet long and about 100 feet high. Each train is equipped with an open observation deck for photographers and those who like to experience the elements while traveling. Remember, the route goes through mountainous areas with unpredictable

weather. The cars aren't heated and warm clothing is necessary even in the summer.

Wiedman says a variety of wildlife can be seen during the ride, including mule deer, elk, antelope, foxes, coyotes, badgers, marmots, squirrels, hawks and golden eagles. But, "You don't see them on every train," he says.

Autumn months offer the best time to ride the rails as the mountain colors change. Wiedman says many riders in the fall are repeaters who want the "colorized" version of the same trip.

Many families with schoolchildren ride the rails during the summer months, while the fall months see a more elderly group on the scenic tour. Wiedman says riders in 1988 were treated to the hoopla of Hollywood, as film crews were shooting train scenes for an Indiana Jones movie. The train has served as set to numerous other Hollywood productions.

During World War II the U.S. government took seven of the railroad's 470-series locomotives to Alaska, where they were needed to haul supplies, arsenals and men. The trains were overworked, poorly maintained and just run to death, never making the return trip to New Mexico.

The Denver & Rio Grande railroad was also essential in the transporting of oil, which was discovered in 1930s about 15 miles west of Chama. The railroad hauled oil on the narrow-gauge route to a refinery in Alamosa, Colo., until about 1964, when it became unprofitable.

For more information call (505) 756-2151. ☀

Above—*The historic narrow-gauge rails bisect some of the most beautiful country on Earth, giving travelers awesome views of the southern Rocky Mountains.*

31

Mark Nohl

The Abiquiú-area museum is expanding its enclosures for bobcats and other larger animals.

Ghost Ranch Living Museum

> *Some (of the animals) were injured, others orphaned and all wouldn't survive if released into the wild.*

by Nancy Harbert

At Ghost Ranch Living Museum, the days begin and end with a cacophony of what comes natural to its inhabitants: wails, screeches, baying.

In between, those residents, ranging from squirrels to raptors to bears, alternate basking in the sun to dozing in the shade. A vibrant panorama of pastel-colored cliffs provides a breathtaking backdrop behind their fenced home.

The museum, situated on U.S. 84, 37 miles north of Española, offers visitors a glimpse of animals that roam the region.

A 4-foot-tall sculptured beaver welcomes you to Beaver National Forest, a replica of a New Mexico national forest. The different life zones found in the state are represented as the forest terrain transforms from high-altitude fir and pine trees to grassland growth.

A stream snakes its way down-ward through this forest exhibit, stocked with rainbow trout and European carp. Human statuettes demonstrate the multiple uses of a national forest, such as fishing, camping, hiking, logging.

A beaver was chosen as this forest's focal point, not merely because of its role in soil and water conservation, but because it symbolizes the settling of the American West. Museum co-founder Arthur Pack believed the lure of beaver pelts attracted Anglo traders and missionaries to the Southwest, expanding the population base from traditional Spanish-speaking people.

Enclosures (museum personnel dislike the word cage) are home to a variety of animals, ranging from eagles to elk that all have names and stories behind them. Some were injured, others orphaned and all wouldn't survive if released

into the wild.

The museum opened its doors in July 1959, the brainstorm of Pack and William Carr. Pack, who owned 23,000 acres that included Ghost Ranch, already had created the Arizona-Sonora Desert Museum outside Tucson. An environmentally conscious man, he wanted to bring an awareness of the natural environment to northern New Mexico. The Ghost Ranch museum was to display plants and animals indigenous to the region for enjoyment and education.

Pack eventually deeded the ranch to the Presbyterian Church, which, through a land transfer, gave the museum to the federal government to be managed by the U.S. Forest Service. Today, the museum also serves as an outreach center for the New Mexico Museum of Natural History, hosting traveling exhibits.

Slappy, the resident beaver, maintains a dwelling bordered by adobe walls and an earth-tone roof. Slappy spends the cold winter months inside the Beaver Museum, which also displays beaver lore and a mineral exhibit.

One of the museum's more well-known residents is Miguel, a great-horned owl. Miguel, who was hit by a car in Española eight years ago, makes regular visits to classrooms throughout central and northern New Mexico with a museum naturalist. The complacent owl also attends museum fund-raising events.

Then there's Oscar and Hortendo, black bears, both orphaned. Oscar was the victim of a rattle-snake bite when he was a small cub.

Just in case visitors get to thinking the animals are touchably cute, a sign posted near the bobcat en-

Above—Inspiring landscapes near Abiquiú, also known as Georgia O'Keeffe Country, serve as the backdrop for the Ghost Ranch Living Museum. Thousands of visitors tour the site annually.

Mark Nohl

closure reads: "Please do not feed your fingers to the animals. Their diet is carefully planned."

The region's spectacular geology is documented in the museum's exhibit, "Up Through The Ages." Each layer of the colorful piñon-dotted cliffs behind the 23-acre museum is described as you walk up a stairway to an observation deck.

The museum also offers a replica of a fire lookout tower and an exhibit hall that includes enclosures for reptiles such as rattlesnakes, bull snakes, a tarantula and the beautifully salmon-speckled Gila monster.

There are also smaller animals, such as raccoons, skunks, foxes, Hugo the badger, and Thorny, the first porcupine born in captivity in New Mexico.

Plans include expanding habitats for bobcats, coyotes, Mexican wolves, mountain lions and black bears.

The museum is open from 8 a.m. to 4:30 p.m. Tuesday through Sunday from September through April and from 8 a.m. to 5:30 p.m. seven days a week during summer months. Admission is free but donations are accepted. For further information, contact Ghost Ranch Living Museum, Abiquiú, N.M. 87510 or call (505) 685-4312.

Above—The wailing of a pack of nighttime coyotes has sent a shiver up the spine of many a person during the centuries. The oft-misunderstood animal also is represented at Ghost Ranch Living Museum.

Mark Nohl

The ruins of both a prehistoric pueblo and a 17th-century mission rise from the rugged landscape at Jémez State Monument, just outside the village of Jémez Springs.

Jémez Country

> *Born of fire, the mountains are now a cool, relatively moist, forested island included in the Santa Fe National Forest, 41,000 acres of which have been designated San Pedro Parks Wilderness.*

by Mike Richie

In the state's north-central mountain region, a huge natural boulevard carves deep into multicolored sandstone and volcanic layers. Magnificent Jémez Canyon winds gently upward for 20 miles connecting two distinct worlds. Sweeping piñon- and juniper-studded steppes transform gradually into spruce and fir forested volcanic peaks.

The Jémez Range receives more than 30 inches of moisture a year compared with 10 for the surrounding plains. Fed by snowmelt and summer thundershowers the Jémez River pours down the canyon creating a swath of deciduous forest or bosque. Cottonwoods and willows, whether vibrant spring green or burnished autumn gold, add extra colors to an already full spectrum. These lush bottomlands have drawn people as far back as 10,000 years. Jémez Pueblo still practices irrigated agriculture in the lower canyon. Pre-Columbian ruins along the river or on high, protected mesatops attest to the continuity of this lifestyle.

Intricately sculpted rock forms, sheltering ramparts, forested rimrock and earth-hewn pueblos add up to classic northern New Mexican landscapes. Beyond the landscape's sheer beauty is a story of nature's immense power. The canyon's 1,200-foot walls are fashioned from thick sandstone beds deposited by wind and water activity during Permian times about 250 million years ago. Uplift and subsequent erosion left an irregular upper surface.

But along the canyon's rimtop, like icing over a very lumpy cake, lies a smooth veneer of volcanic rock. The light grey tuff, or compacted ash, forms the periphery of a massive volcanic eruption that

35

Mark Nohl   Mark Nohl

made the more recent Mount St. Helens explosion resemble a flaring wooden match in comparison. The bulk of the activity occurred recently by geological standards, just more than a million years ago. Thousand-foot-thick ash deposits covered 400 square miles, building up a huge plateau that now forms the base of the Jémez Mountains.

Following the canyon north toward the mountains and the eruption's core, the ash layer thickens. Above the town of Jémez Springs the east fork's walls become completely volcanic. The upper canyon opens suddenly onto an expanse of partially forested meadows known as the Valle Grande. This circular, 15-mile-diameter depression along with four sister *valles* is the heart of the largest system of volcanic craters or caldera in the world.

Eight peaks, more than 10,000 feet high, tower above the Valle Grande. The two highest, Santa Clara at 11,561 feet and Redondo at 11,254 feet, are secondary cinder cones that grew from the crater floor. Other high peaks form the caldera's eastern and southwestern rim. Beneath the surface, groundwater flows through hot rock, heating up to 500 degrees Fahrenheit in some areas. Numerous hot springs bubble to the surface, giving the Jémez its unique and well-known character.

Born of fire, the mountains are now a cool, relatively moist, forested island included in the Santa Fe National Forest, 41,000 acres of which have been designated San Pedro Parks Wilderness. Runoff pours down the crater sides forming numerous canyons like Alamo, Frijoles, Church and San Antonio. Filled with natural alcoves, amphitheaters and lush vegetation pockets, these canyons contain some of

the most beautiful spots in the region.

In New Mexico it's possible to choose a climate by choosing an elevation. Where the desert meets the mountains in the canyons the balance is ideal. Numerous and varied pre-Columbian populations, especially in the Pueblo period between A.D. 1200-1500, took advantage of this fact. Their ruins blend with the landscapes, a reminder of how closely humankind and the natural world were once linked. Bandelier National Monument, Jémez State Monument, which has one of the oldest missions in the country, and Guisewa Pueblo, the Jémez Indians' ancestral home, along with the more primitive Puyé ruins represent only a few well-known sites. Ancient hunting paths crisscross the caldera. Areas such as Obsidian Ridge and Flint Mountain pro-

vided important materials for tools and weapons. Many high peaks had shrines intact as recently as 50 years ago. Santa Clara, the highest, goes by the name of *Tschicoma* and was considered the center of the Tewa Pueblo world. Five present-day pueblos encircle the caldera's eastern flanks.

Forested peaks, extensive high meadows, dramatic canyons and rock forms, rivers, waterfalls, hot springs, pre-Columbian ruins, living pueblos, ghost towns, mountain villages—the Jémez Mountains contain all the elements needed to make a distinct New Mexican environment. ✹

Mark Nohl

The Overlook Trail offers cross-country skiers excellent views from the Jémez Mountains.

Jémez Cross-country Trails

by Linda Vozar Sweet

In the Jémez Mountains wildflowers bloom late into fall and snow clings to the earth long into spring. Abundant cross-country skiing and hiking trails weave throughout these mountains, but four areas—Upper Frijoles, Las Conchas, East Fork Ridge and Redondo—offer varied terrain and superb views. At their farthest points the well-marked trails on N.M. 4 span just 15 miles; an avid skier or hiker could easily explore two of them in a weekend. Each one renders a different visual experience.

A good place to start is the Upper Frijoles ski and hiking trail. Located in the northwest corner of Bandelier National Monument, the two loop trails offer three overlooks of Frijoles Canyon where the wandering ancestors of the Cochití Indians carved kivas and cliff dwellings into the pink-colored volcanic tuff below. Against a cloudless sky, a vista of desert and mountains all meet in rosy tints of blues and greens.

The gently rolling terrain of the Upper Frijoles trail makes this an excellent spot for the inexperienced skier. The short loop trail is nearly a flat glide for the entire 2.4 miles. The danger of colliding with another skier is considerably reduced on these trails. Blue and orange markers send skiers traveling in the same direction. Maps available at the trailhead show the routes and overlook spots into this canyon explored in the 19th century by Adolf Bandelier.

Continue south for 7.6 miles through the expansive meadows of the Valle Grande and you'll reach the Las Conchas trailhead just beyond Las Conchas campground, where the road crosses the East Fork of the Jémez River. This trail

courses over frozen, trout-filled waters and follows the canyon bottom's narrow meadows, brimming with wildflowers in the spring. You're inside a canyon, gazing up 300-foot, buff-colored walls that rise into stark grandeur. This is probably the most spectacular trail to ski or hike. The canyon walls, like vast pillars of landscape, dominate this trail.

Be certain, however, that the many ice and snow bridges crossing the stream can bear your weight. A dip in the stream on a winter day could cause hypothermia. Nature lovers can find a green bed of watercress growing year-round in a warm spring at the spot where the trail boxes into a steep incline to the top of East Fork Ridge, an ascent not recommended for skiers. The trail is 3.6 miles round-trip—worth every glide.

A more wildernesslike tour is found 3.7 miles farther south at the west trailhead of East Fork Ridge Trail. This rigorous trail, a challenge for the intermediate skier, traverses a forested ridgetop of pines, fir and spruce. Be on the lookout for elk and deer prints that cross the trail and disappear in silvery groves of aspen.

When tired, you can rest for a while on a fallen tree in the cold, deep silence of the forest and glimpse the frosty peak of Redondo glinting through spindly ponderosa pines. At a wide clearing, 2.5 miles from the highway, much of the East Fork Canyon is visible as is a broad view of Redondo Peak. Indians say the shape of an eagle can be seen on the peak. Plenty of blue diamonds mark this trail, about one every 40 feet.

At Redondo campground, 4

Above—*Classic wintertime forest scenes always appear to those hardy souls who cross-country ski the Jémez Mountains, where abundant snowpack usually is the norm.*

39

David Ponton

Above—*A couple of Nordic skiers glide past skeletal aspen trees standing amongst tall evergreens deep in the Jémez Mountains.*

miles to the south, trails more appropriate for families with children curve through the forest, while the advanced skier might want to try the narrow trails that cling to the rims of two craters. Park at the Jémez Canyon Overloók parking area, then cross N.M. 4, and ski north a short distance to Redondo campground.

Most trails in this location follow the wide, gentle grade of logging roads.

Experienced skiers will want to ski Crater Spur Trail, notable because it skirts two bowl-shaped craters related to the volcanic activity common in the Jémez Mountains a million years ago. To find the tree-filled craters, ski a quarter-mile east from the trailhead and follow the trail marked with blue diamonds. Late in the season you can rest in the cove of warm, dry pine needles along the south-facing edge of the craters where the snow

has melted.

Skiers and hikers will find many more cross-country trails in the Jémez Mountains, not just the four mentioned here. Double-check maps and speak with local authorities to avoid skiing on private land. No matter what the season, the beauty of these meadows, plateaus, canyons and ridgetop clearings remains as constant as the sunset. ☀

40

Mark Nohl

The interior of the Chapel of Our Lady of Light, more commonly known as Loretto Chapel.

Loretto Chapel

Whether or not the visitor believes there was a miracle, the staircase remains a marvel.

by Emily Drabanski

Every year thousands of people travel to Santa Fe to visit a small, Gothic chapel on the Old Santa Fe Trail. Tucked in the back corner of the chapel an elegant, wooden staircase twists like a coiled spring with 33 steps to the choir loft. It is the legend of the "miraculous" staircase that brings people inside this small, French-inspired chapel.

Some believe it truly is a miracle, others view it with respect and awe of the mastery of carpentry integral in building the steep, swirling staircase.

The Chapel of Our Lady of the Light, known more commonly as Loretto Chapel, was built for the Sisters of Loretto in 1873. The nuns had left Kentucky and made an arduous trip across the Mississippi River and the West to establish a convent in Santa Fe under the direction of Archbishop Jean Baptiste Lamy. They would later establish a school for girls that operated until 1968.

The archbishop, the subject of Willa Cather's novel *Death Comes for the Archbishop*, stirred much controversy by his repression of local customs, including native architecture. It was at his request that the chapel be built in a Gothic style reminiscent of the Sainte-Chapelle in Paris. French and Italian stone masons were brought in for the project and they would later build the St. Francis Cathedral several blocks away.

The construction took five years. The result was an elegant chapel complete with a beautiful choir loft. But when the chapel was finished, there was no way to climb to the choir loft. There are several interpretations of why this occurred. In that time most boys and men went to choir lofts by ladder, but

41

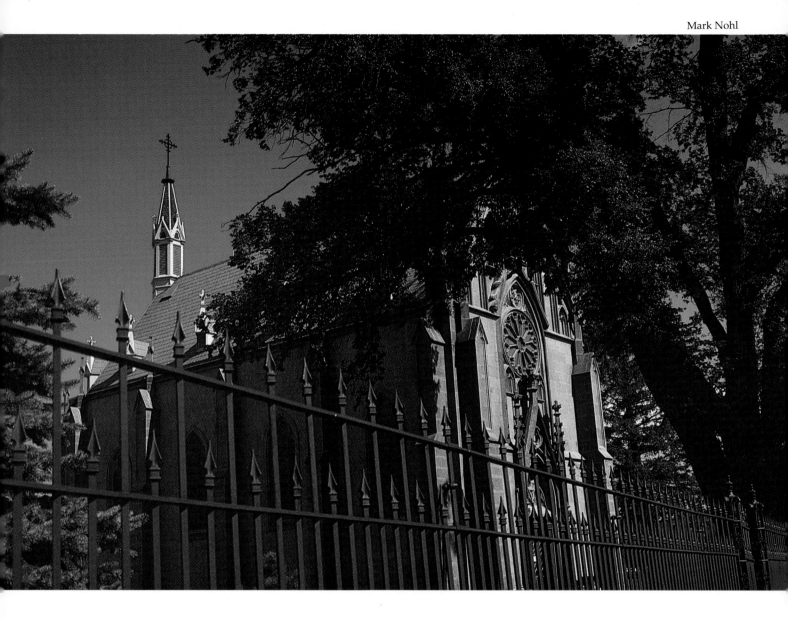

Above—*Loretto Chapel was built in 1873, about 21 years after the Sisters of Loretto opened a boarding school for girls called Loretto Academy that lasted until 1968.*

the nuns did not want to climb in their long habits nor ask the young girls at the school to ascend such a tall ladder.

Alice Bullock, in the Sunstone booklet *Loretto and the Miraculous Staircase*, tells the story of how the young, French architect who led the construction died before the project was completed. Some say the architect became too friendly with the wife of Lamy's nephew. This led to gossip and the wife moved into a room at the Exchange Hotel, located on the site of La Fonda today. When Lamy's nephew saw the architect leave his wife's room, he drew a pistol and shot him.

It was possible the builders did not know the architect's plan for getting to the choir loft and there was confusion among the crew members, who either spoke French, Italian, Spanish or English.

Other carpenters were summoned but they could not offer a solution. The Sisters of Loretto, distressed by the dilemma, decided to pray a novena through St. Joseph, the patron saint of carpenters.

According to the legend, on the ninth day, a gray-haired man arrived with a donkey and offered his assistance. To this day, the carpenter, who left without payment, has remained unidentified. Many who visit the chapel, as 10-year-old Danielle Arsola has done several times, think it is possible St. Joseph built the stairway.

"It's amazing because he only used three tools—a saw, a T square and a hammer," she says. That is the story often told at the chapel. According to reports the nuns passed down through the years, they also saw the unidentified carpenter soaking wood in tubs of water.

42

Mary J. Straw in her book, *Loretto and The Sisters and Their Santa Fe Chapel*, says several people have claimed their grandfathers or other relatives built the staircase. None of these reports were ever verified.

Whether or not the visitor believes there was a miracle, the staircase remains a marvel. With its two complete 360-degree turns, it's no wonder the nuns say that the first ones to climb to the choir loft were so frightened by the dizzying turns that they had to come down on their hands and knees. After several years of use, it was determined that a handrailing was essential. The handrailing itself is a masterpiece of carpentry.

The staircase withstood more than 85 years of continuous use. Today, in the interest of safety and historical preservation, it is used only on special occasions.

The Sisters of Loretto sold the property in 1968. The chapel was deconsecrated and now is under the ownership and management of the adjacent Inn at Loretto.

Jim Bagby, general manager of the Inn, estimates about 2,200 people visit the chapel every day. The chapel in the 200 block of Old Santa Fe Trail is open 9 a.m. to 5 p.m. every day except Christmas. The Inn also rents out the chapel for special occasions, such as concerts and weddings. For more information, call the chapel at (505) 984-7971. To inquire about special events, call the Inn's sales office at (505) 988-5531. ✺

Above—*The afternoon light creates frolicking shadows on the Loretto Chapel while St. Francis Cathedral looms in the background. The two structures represent Archbishop Jean Baptiste Lamy's aggressive policy to stray from local religious customs and architecture.*

Mark Nohl

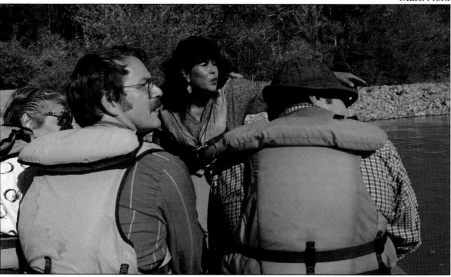

Marian Naranjo draws on her river surroundings to explain Santa Clara Pueblo culture.

Santa Clara Rafting

> *"What we offer is a chance for visitors to meet the people, to share our lives and experiences. . . ."*

by Jon Bowman

In its native Tewa language, Santa Clara Pueblo goes by the name *Kha'po* or Singing Water. The name celebrates the Río Grande, which snakes leisurely through the pueblo, meandering south past Black Mesa, an immense, pocked outcropping of volcanic rock with spiritual significance for the Santa Clara.

Flanked by cottonwoods and Russian olives, this peaceful stretch of the river provides sanctuary for abundant waterfowl, including the majestic blue heron. In earlier years, the area was off-limits to most visitors. But with a new tour launched by the Española-area pueblo, visitors now can soak up the serene surroundings while floating down the Río Grande on a raft.

The river cruise represents a marked change of pace from the days when busloads of tourists would pull into the pueblo, possibly into someone's front yard, and stare out the windows as residents made their daily rounds.

By initiating the raft trips, Santa Clara has taken more direct control over its tourism trade while at the same time offering visitors more intimate contact than before. An Indian guide leads each excursion, discussing the pueblo's culture, history and beliefs. At the end of the six-mile float, passengers are greeted by Santa Clara elders bearing Indian tacos and home-cooked delicacies for a traditional feast.

"What we offer is a chance for visitors to meet the people, to share our lives and experiences through our guides and senior citizens," says former Santa Clara business manager Joe Baca, who helped organize the tours.

He adds that other pueblos are studying the operation so that

they, too, can increase revenue from tourism without creating undue interference in the day-to-day lives of tribal members.

Marian Naranjo, Santa Clara's most experienced raft guide, knows every bend of the river. She draws on the sights around her—a circling hawk, a muskrat den, the towering Black Mesa—as the starting point for her many stories.

She talks of Avanyu, the Water Serpent who protects the river. Santa Clara's religion, she explains, is based on the natural world. She tells how spiritual beliefs shape everyday life, from the division of the pueblo into kiva clans to the choice of designs used on Santa Clara's famed black and red pottery.

Her presentation is anything but dry. A warm, outgoing woman, Naranjo jokes casually with the raft passengers, informing a New York couple that Santa Clara perfected the condominium centuries ago with the cliff dwellings at Puyé Cliffs.

Every once in a while, she cuts short her talk to help the pilot steer clear of a sandbar or to duck an oncoming branch jutting out over the river. The Río Grande flows gently here, but there are occasional ripples of current and underwater snags to circumnavigate.

Visitors tired of the hype and hustle of standard tours give the Santa Clara raft trips high marks as a relaxing, informative experience. "It's peaceful and very lovely," says Ann Tesler of North Miami Beach, Fla. "When you have a true native speaking to you, you feel a lot closer to what you're seeing."

"Most tours are very structured, very commercial," says Floyd Glinert of Englewood Cliffs, N.J. "What makes this one special is that it is so informal. You can learn

Above—Black Mesa overshadows these Santa Clara-sponsored rafters navigating the Río Grande. The mound is much the focal point of mythology and religion of Tewa Indians who call it toonyopeeng ya, or "very spotted mountains."

Above—*Black Mesa at dusk. The hill served as haven for Indians from San Ildefonso who took refuge on top from Spanish soldiers who besieged them there at the close of the Pueblo Revolt. Don Diego de Vargas made three unsuccessful attempts to assault it. The site is off-limits to visitors.*

while you enjoy it. You get to see the sights, but beyond that, you come away with a real good perspective and feeling about the people."

Santa Clara lies directly south of Española along N.M. 30, about 25 miles north of Santa Fe. Raft trip reservations may be placed through Singing Water Tours at (505) 753-9663 or by contacting Santa Fe Detours in the hotel lobby at La Fonda, off the Santa Fe Plaza. The company maintains a toll-free number, (800) DETOURS, for out-of-state calls and may be reached in state at (505) 983-6565.

The entire tour takes about five hours, including time on the water, dinner and round-trip transportation from Santa Fe. Rafting professionals from the Southwest Wilderness Center accompany each river trip to ensure safety. ◈

Water courses through a channel cutting into Soda Dam.

Soda Dam

> *As the water cools on the earth's surface, the minerals precipitate to form the travertine deposits that have grown over thousands of years to create the so-called dam.*

by Linda Vozar Sweet

One of the most mysterious spots in the Jémez Mountains, and one of the most accessible, is an extraordinary piece of geology known as Soda Dam. What makes it so mysterious is its strange mushroom-shaped exterior and the caves in and around Soda Dam that create a mystical aura.

The most interesting cave often is overlooked by visitors who venture no farther than the side of the road for a photo. Getting inside the cave requires some agility, though there are plenty of handholds to help you along the way.

Once inside, the underlying reality of Soda Dam is suddenly revealed. A large fountain of wavy travertine rock holds a quiet pool of warm, shimmering water and you get the impression you've been transported into the realm of dreams or fairy tales. Thousands of layers of calcium carbonate surround you. It's like being inside the bones of the earth.

The water spills silently down the fountain and flows out into daylight, then trickles into the Jémez River roaring through the dam below. The atmosphere is supernatural, especially in winter when vapors rise from the cave and all around the snow-covered dam, where warm water emerges.

A mile-and-a-half north of the village of Jémez Springs on N.M. 4, Soda Dam was formed by hot springs emerging from a fault zone. Looking west you can see the same mushroom-shaped formations of earlier dams created centuries ago. In technical terms, the dam is a deposit of travertine rock built from hot mineral water carrying calcium carbonate, not sodium bicarbonate as the name implies. As the water cools on the earth's

Above—*Swimmers find the waters of Soda Dam pleasing in the warmer months, while warm water pools create good conditions for wading.*

surface, the minerals precipitate to form the travertine deposits that have grown over thousands of years to create the so-called dam.

In warmer months the Jémez River at Soda Dam is a popular swimming hole. More daring individuals can swim to a ledge behind the waterfall where the river tunnels through the dam.

A hike up the west canyon on a steep, well-worn trail reveals a different view of Soda Dam and another cave. This overlook provides a good view of the Jémez River flowing calmly behind Soda Dam just before it gushes dramatically through the dam's opening. If you continue hiking about 100 feet, you'll find a large cave known as Jémez Cave, once a warehouse of archaeological treasures.

In his book *Exploring The Jemez Country*, Roland A. Pettitt says that it was used by some of the earliest

prehistoric human inhabitants of the valley. "The first occupancy dates from 2500 B.C. and continued through the early Spanish era," Pettitt said. "Indian artifacts from the cave include prayer sticks, rabbit clubs and *atlatls* [hand-held sticks for hurling spears]. Also discovered was the mummified body of an Indian baby wrapped in a blanket woven from a single 320-foot-long strand of twisted turkey-feather down."

Back on the road along the west canyon wall, you'll spot more hot water emerging from older dams and flowing over emerald green algae into pools alongside the road. It also bubbles out of the ground here. Too small for bathing but just the right size for wading, these pools entice tourists to soak their feet in the soothing warm water, believed by many to have healing properties.

48

Mark Nohl

If you stand on the highest point just south of the official scenic marker, you can see the foundation of the old bridge that crossed the Jémez River before the 1950s when N.M. 4 was still a dirt road. And if you walk a short distance farther south, you can make out the old road that used to follow the east side of the river at Soda Dam before the new highway was built.

Just downstream from the dam along the west side of the road rise steep salmon-colored granite bluffs that are about 1,450 to 1,730 years old. After a summer rain, the bluffs turn brilliant shades of pink and orange and purple. Studded with yucca, juniper and cholla, these ancient cliffs offer another impressive site to travelers.

N.M. 4 is a highway of geological wonders. In addition to Soda Dam and its various caves, there is Battleship Rock four miles to the north, with picnic facilities at its base. Farther up the road you can sometimes spot Redondo Peak. At an elevation of 11,254 feet, it is one of the state's highest mountains. If you stay on N.M. 4 you can see other spectacular sites such as Jémez Falls and Valle Grande caldera. Just a mile south of Soda Dam is Jémez State Monument.

When you visit Soda Dam, remember to tread gently over its surface. Slow erosion occurs each time a visitor stops to explore this geological wonder. It's a spot sure to activate the imagination. ❦

Above—Mineral-rich waters of Soda Dam.

Hikers must tread a well-worn pathway to reach Tsankawi Ruins, an offshoot of Bandelier National Monument near White Rock.

Tsankawi Ruins

> *Looking over the small clearing and watching brush and piñon trees wave in the wind, it's hard to believe that this once was the site of a thriving Indian community . . . .*

by Alex Parsons

Tsankawi Ruins, near Los Alamos, provides a look back into the history of the Río Grande Anasazi. Here, evidence remains of the intimate relationship that existed between the land and the prehistoric precursors of the Pueblo Indians.

The site stretches out on the Pajarito Plateau, nestled among the Jémez Mountains. The plateau was created more than one million years ago during the formation of one of the world's largest volcanoes. Its eruptions blackened the skies of New Mexico with ash that coated the surrounding landscape in thick layers, drowning all life. Eventually, the flora and fauna returned, and the area became the home of Native Americans looking for good hunting and farming grounds. Pueblos were built, and many, such as Tsankawi (tsank-ah-WEE), were later abandoned, leaving decaying ruins spread throughout the mesatops.

The soft ash from the eruptions easily eroded. By the time Indians began to settle the area, steep-walled canyons, small caves and high mesas had been carved into the landscape. The Anasazis enlarged the caves to provide room for shelter and storage. In addition, the high mesas were easily defended, making them perfect sites for pueblos.

The Anasazi inhabited Tsankawi from about A.D. 1400 to the late 1500s. Although it is unexcavated, the ruin is believed to have been abandoned because of drought and soil depletion, which forced the inhabitants to leave the stone walls of the pueblo to deteriorate into the jumbled ruins that lie atop the mesa.

The drive to Tsankawi is almost as enjoyable as the hike through

the ruins. If you drive north from Santa Fe, U.S. 84-285 passes by both Tesuque and Pojoaque pueblos. In Pojoaque veer west onto N.M. 502, which rolls over a dusty New Mexico landscape of volcanic tuff dotted with gnarled piñon trees. Later, the highway crosses through a verdant green ribbon of cottonwoods marking the path of the Río Grande. Farther along, the road ascends into the mountainous Jémez area. High mesas enclose the highway on either side, their sheer walls broken periodically by deep canyons. Tsankawi lies amid this striking landscape, marked only by a small, lightly graveled parking lot on the east side of the road.

The one-and-a-half-mile trail that weaves its way through the mesa and ruins has been carved down to a depth of more than a foot in some stretches from extensive use. The path leads through a

narrow cleft in the rocks below the mesatop. Climbing through the cleft can be tricky, as it is fairly steep and barely over a foot wide in points. The top of the mesa offers a panoramic view of the Pajarito Plateau. Surrounding mesas stand out in bright contrast to the dark green of the vegetation, their raw cliff walls illuminated brightly by the sun.

Toward the eastern edge of the mesa lie the remnants of Tsankawi. Along the trail, dusty potsherds of different designs and colors can be seen. Gray pumice blocks of uniform size dot a clearing, resting in jumbled piles. Ragweed grows up around the edges of the stones and the dull green of chamisa is everywhere.

The various humps and depressions used to be a village of about 350 rooms, up to 3 stories high. Close inspection reveals two shal-

Above—Scenery surrounding the Tsankawi Ruins makes the area a delight to photographers. The well-worn foot trail is evident to the right.

low depressions that used to be kivas located in what was the plaza area of the pueblo.

Looking over the small clearing and watching brush and piñon trees wave in the wind, it's hard to believe this once was the site of a thriving Indian community that conducted a brisk trade in tools, pottery, blankets and other goods, and farmed the canyon below.

Aside from the ruins on the mesa, there are a number of cliff-side cave dwellings, petroglyphs and a beautiful view of the Pa-jarito Plateau, surrounded by the Sangre de Cristo Mountains to the east and the Jémez Mountains to the west.

To get to Tsankawi take N.M. 502 out of Pojoaque and head to-ward Los Alamos. Then turn south onto N.M. 4 and head toward White Rock. Just before N.M. 4 intersects with the Los Alamos truck route, you will see a small parking lot on the east side of the road and a brown sign reading "Tsankawi."

A National Park Service ranger collects fees on weekends. A camp-ground host occupies the ruins during the summer to answer questions. No pets or nighttime hiking are allowed. For more infor-mation call (505) 672-3861. ✤

Above—Soft volcanic ash formed nearly a million years ago made it possible for Indians to carve caves for shelter and storage.

Mark Nohl

Rows of wooden frame houses still line the streets of Madrid, a ghost town alive again.

Turquoise Trail

Cerrillos still looks like an Old West movie set and indeed Hollywood has returned here many times to film.

by Emily Drabanski

Getting there is half the fun, they say. So the next time you travel between Albuquerque and Santa Fe take the back road on N.M. 14 if you're looking for fun along the way.

The winding road will lead you through spectacular mountain terrain to historic mining towns. Along the way you'll have a chance to stop for refreshments at quiet cafes and lively taverns and be invited to browse through art galleries and antique shops.

The Turquoise Trail Association, a group representing businesses along the route, suggests beginning your tour by getting off at Exit 175 of Interstate 40 east of Albuquerque to travel N.M. 14.

Cedar Crest and Sandía Park offer mountain terrain on the east side of the Sandías. Many visitors cruise to the wooded area to dine at several popular restaurants.

At the Sandía Crest turnoff, you can venture off N.M. 14 to N.M. 536 to take a breathtaking ride to the summit along the Sandía Crest National Scenic Byway. In the summer bring your hiking boots to find a cool respite in the towering ponderosa pine. En route stop at the Tinkertown Miniature Village, just a mile from the turnoff. The miniature Old West town is open from April through November.

Downhill and cross-country skiers will find what they're looking for at the Sandía Peak Ski Area. In the summer you can take a heart-pounding ride on the chair lifts. Six miles farther and you'll reach the crest with spectacular views at 10,678 feet. Stretch your legs on the hiking trails in this mountain terrain or browse through the shop and restaurant at the crest before beginning your descent.

As you leave the cutoff and head

Above—Tourist-oriented shops have replaced hardware and general merchandise stores in historic Cerrillos, once a booming mining camp, then ghost town and now a thriving haven for visitors and artists.

north on N.M. 14 the terrain changes near the foothills of the Ortíz Mountains. Junipers, piñon, sage and cholla cactus punctuate the roadside into a mineral-rich area that once supported three booming mine towns.

Golden, named for a gold rush in the 1800s, once supported saloons and a stock exchange. Now, Golden's most famous landmark is a small church resting quietly among the cholla cactus.

About eight miles down the road is Madrid with its rows of old, wooden frame houses. Coal, an important fuel in the 1880s, led to the growth of this town. Following World War II the coal demand lessened, leading to the collapse and abandonment of the town.

In the 1950s the owner tried to sell the whole town and had no takers. In the mid-70s, he sold off the houses individually. He sold

them for a song, although there was hardly anything left to hum about. The old frame houses had dilapidated roofs and were missing walls. But a lot of sweat, hammers and nails have restored a number of homes—many filled with folks seeking an alternative lifestyle. Still, some houses stand empty.

You can descend into an old mine shaft at the Old Coal Mine Museum and see mining relics. Adjacent is the Mine Shaft Tavern, serving spirits, food and entertainment with the flavor of an Old West saloon. The Turquoise Trail theater frequently offers productions in the adjacent space. In the summer, melodramas attract crowds booing at the villains. Across the road there's a snack and gift shop in an old train car.

Many of Madrid's newcomers sell arts and crafts. The former

company store that dominates the main drag now houses four distinct shops along a wooden boardwalk. You'll find a pottery studio, a classy art gallery, an import store and country store. Jewelers, potters and weavers often can be found working in other shops.

A few miles from Madrid is Cerrillos (little hills). In these hills, turquoise, gold, silver, lead and zinc were extracted. In its heyday during the 1880s, the town had as many as 27 saloons and four hotels. The Palace Hotel welcomed guests such as Thomas A. Edison, Ulysses S. Grant and Gov. L. Bradford Prince. Only rubble of the hotel remains.

Cerrillos still looks like an Old West movie set and indeed Hollywood has returned here many times to film. Most recently, the movie *Young Guns* was shot here.

Many of the old buildings are private homes, but you're welcome to browse in the shops around town. You'll find antique stores and a homegrown museum and petting zoo. The town also has its own down-home celebration every June, Fiesta Primavera. As you leave town, a sign bids *"Hasta la Vista."*

North along N.M. 14, the Old West town fades in your memory as the hillsides are dotted with newer adobe and frame homes.

The end of the Turquoise Trail will take you into Santa Fe. Or return down N.M. 14 or take the faster route along Interstate 25 back to Albuquerque. When planning your trip, allow plenty of time. The winding road calls for alert driving. For more information about the Turquoise Trail, write to the association at P.O. Box 693, Albuquerque, N.M. 87103.

Above left—This church at Golden dominates the landscape of the once-bustling town, founded in 1879 as a center for gold mining. A settlement named Real de San Francisco previously occupied the site of Golden. *Left*—Ruins typical of New Mexican architecture dot the roadsides of the Turquoise Trail.

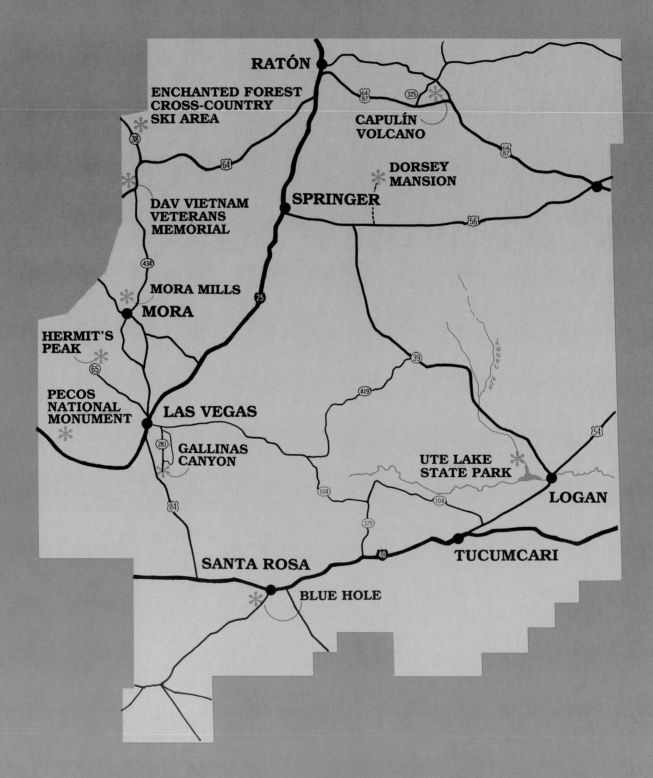

RATÓN

ENCHANTED FOREST
CROSS-COUNTRY
SKI AREA

CAPULÍN
VOLCANO

DORSEY
MANSION

DAV VIETNAM
VETERANS
MEMORIAL

SPRINGER

MORA MILLS
MORA

HERMIT'S
PEAK

PECOS
NATIONAL
MONUMENT

LAS VEGAS

GALLINAS
CANYON

UTE LAKE
STATE PARK

LOGAN

SANTA ROSA

TUCUMCARI

BLUE HOLE

Mark Nohl

Scuba divers from several states are drawn by the crystal-clear waters of Santa Rosa's Blue Hole.

Blue Hole

Having its own aquatic environment of textures, sands, snails, plants and fish, Blue Hole has been called Nature's Largest Fishbowl.

by Emily Drabanski

It's hard to believe a land of cactus, cattle and little rainfall also could hold the best scuba-diving waters around. But Santa Rosa, a town with a population of about 2,200 on the eastern plains of New Mexico, has become a gathering place for hundreds of divers every weekend year-round.

From as far away as Virginia, scuba divers flock to what is known as Blue Hole. "I spend a lot of time driving to and from this place. It's the best anywhere," one diver from Kansas says.

Situated close to the Pecos River, Blue Hole is one of many lakes in the area. Small and unpretentious, it is in the center of town near a city park. And it's really just a hole. Rimmed by sandstone, Blue Hole measures only 80 feet in diameter. It drops another 80 feet straight down. Compared with other diving spots, it isn't large. What lures so many to Blue Hole is its clarity.

Artesian fed, the water is replaced every six hours at a rate of 3,000 gallons per minute; the water is always fresh and clear. When the water is extremely clear, divers at the bottom can see people walking around above. Night dives also are popular. On cloudless nights, the moon and stars can be seen from the bottom of Blue Hole. Because the water continuously seeps in from underground, the water remains a constant 64 degrees. Even though it can be a little chilly afterward, a few hardy souls dive Blue Hole during the dead of winter.

The terrain beneath the surface varies remarkably, with some walls containing a black alkaline deposit that resembles coral. A large amphitheater along one wall, its floor layered with fine silt, sometimes seems to have no bottom.

Above—Centuries of tradition and period architecture are a common site throughout the Santa Rosa area in the northeast.

At the 80-foot mark, a small opening serves as the entrance to the vast cave system beyond. But a grate has been installed due to a few unlucky divers who set out to explore the maze of underwater caves and got lost. Catfish and crawdads live in the water and have become rather blasè about divers. Having its own aquatic environment of textures, sands, snails, plants and fish, Blue Hole has been called Nature's Largest Fishbowl.

People have been drawn to Blue Hole for quite a while. With petroglyphs painted on cliffs nearby and arrowheads still commonly found in the area, the Plains Indians frequented Blue Hole. But legend has it that the Indians merely stopped for water or to perform ceremonies; they never settled in the area because they believed the land was sinking. Due to the porosity of the ground, some of Santa Rosa's citizens continue to believe this.

In the 1880s, settlers in the Santa Rosa area used Blue Hole as a source of drinking water. Handmade chisels, square wagon-wheel nails and coins dating back to the late 1800s have been brought up from the depths.

In 1930, the U.S. Fish and Wildlife Service tapped the waters of Blue Hole for a fish hatchery. Ten ponds were constructed near the hole and thousands of pounds of bluegill, bass, catfish and crappie were raised. Then in 1970, the federal government closed down the Santa Rosa operation and turned Blue Hole over to the city.

Its popularity almost assures that Blue Hole will remain a diving area for a long time to come. Some days as many as 200 scuba divers have been counted in the water at the same time.

Diving clubs and schools use the hole for beginning instruction and safety drills. Wet suits are required. A diving shop, located at the lake, rents complete equipment sets as well as separate items. Air is also available. Permits are required and can be bought at the Santa Rosa Police Department. Divers must be certified or must be accompanied by a certified, insured instructor.

Each year a Scubafest is conducted, with a treasure hunt, search and salvage, and navigation course.

Blue Hole is easy to find. Follow the main business loop off Interstate 40, turn south on N.M. 91 and drive four blocks to La Pradira Avenue. Turn left and follow the signs for another five blocks. ✦

Above—Most visitors to Blue Hole and the Santa Rosa area are sure to catch a glimpse of nearby Puerto de Luna. Villagers claim that explorer Francisco Vázquez de Coronado camped at the site and named it "gateway of the moon" because of a narrow gap in the mountains near the community that allows the moon to shine on a river valley during certain times of the month.

Mark Nohl

When the weather is good, visitors can look out over the plains of Colorado, Texas, Oklahoma and Kansas from the summit of Capulín Volcano National Monument near Ratón.

Capulín Volcano

> *The view from atop Capulín is breathtaking, a striking composition of volcanic mountains dotted with lava-capped hills and mesas.*

by Laura Shubert

Have you ever wondered what it's like to walk inside a volcano and explore it?

You don't have to travel to far-away lands for such an adventure. At Capulín Volcano National Monument, just 30 miles east of Ratón, visitors can hike in and around the crater of a volcanic mountain.

Capulín Volcano became a national monument in 1906; it is contained in an area slightly larger than one square mile. *Capulín* is Spanish for chokecherry, a plant found in great abundance in and around the park.

As early as 10,000 years ago, volcanic ash and lava would have been part of this landscape, and even though the volcanic cinder cone now is extinct, the landscape shows evidence of its tumultuous history. The view from atop Capulín is breathtaking, a striking composition of volcanic mountains dotted with lava-capped hills and mesas.

Capulín, which rises more than 1,000 feet from its base, is the cone of a volcano that was active during one of the last stages of a great period of volcanism that started two million years earlier. What is particularly striking about Capulín is its graceful symmetry. The majority of active volcanoes spew lava over the top of their rims, changing their conelike shape. In Capulín's case, lava flowed from side vents, leaving its conical shape intact. Capulín is technically termed a cinder cone volcano, comprised of ash, rock and loose cinders. These materials were thrown out of the volcano only to fall back upon the vent, forming the cone-shaped mound that now is Capulín.

Be sure to take time to stop at the visitor center to view a short movie

on Capulín's history and pick up brochures on touring the monument. Behind the visitor center is a short nature trail that is paved and accessible to the handicapped. Along the trail you will find information on the flora and fauna within the monument and learn about volcanic phenomena known as squeeze-ups. The rivers of lava that once coursed closely beneath the ground caused the squeeze-ups. Hot lava pushed through the weak spots of earth and created unusual lava formations.

From the visitor center, a two-mile road snakes around Capulín Volcano and ends at a parking lot where two self-guided tours begin. Crater Rim Trail circles one mile around the rim of the crater. On clear days, hikers can see four surrounding states from the highest point on this trail. The second trail, about 350 yards long, allows visi-

tors to walk down into the volcano and examine the crater.

Capulín Volcano is historically important. Arrowheads and fire rings indicate that Indians hunted and camped there. The town of Folsom and the famous Folsom site, where artifacts of prehistoric man were found, are nine miles north of the monument.

Wagon trains traveling along the Cimarron branch of the Santa Fe Trail and cowboys moving cattle used Capulín Volcano as a landmark. In the latter 19th century, the notorious train robber Black Jack Ketchum and his gang roamed the area around Capulín and Folsom.

It is difficult to say what time of year is best to visit Capulín. During a normally short spring, the land turns a vivid green speckled with an array of wildflowers, including bluebonnets, Indian paintbrush and many plants of the *Sene-*

Above—*The geology surrounding Capulín Mountain is historically dynamic. Geologists estimate that the extinct volcano was born at least 7,000 years ago and dates from the last stages of volcanic activity along the fault lines of North and South America.*

W.P. Fleming

Above—*Rising 1,000 feet from its base and reaching an elevation of 8,215 feet, Capulín Mountain became a national monument in 1916. The crater on top measures a mile in circumference and drops about 415 feet.*

cio family. Springtime also welcomes the return of wild turkey and deer. For bird-watchers both spring and fall offer the best opportunity to view mountain bluebirds, grosbeak, finches and warblers.

Summer brings the return of an unlikely, yet profuse seasonal resident: the ladybug. From early June through late August, swarms of ladybugs make their home on the east side of the Crater Rim Trail and park officials aren't sure what brings the ladybugs back every year.

Summer visitors who spend the night in the town of Capulín can look forward to historical talks as rangers give informal talks around a roaring bonfire that warms the cool mountain evenings.

Don't worry if you can't get to the monument during the warmer months, for winter, too, is a magic

time. Although there is not much wildlife to be seen, plants and trees are covered with a crystal frost that offers photo opportunities of the dramatic winter landscape. All trails are open in during the winter except when heavy snow makes them inaccessible.

Capulín Volcano National Monument, located three miles from the town of Capulín, is open year-round and daytime hours are extended in the summer. A fee is charged per vehicle. Camping areas can be found in the nearby communities of Capulín, Folsom, Des Moines and Ratón. Des Moines, Ratón and Clayton offer overnight accommodations.

To get to the park from Ratón and Interstate 25, travel 30 miles east on U.S. 64/87. From Clayton take U.S. 64/87 west for 58 miles.

Mark Nohl

The 2-story Dorsey Mansion stands as a monument to a powerful wheeler-dealer and the rough-and-tumble era of New Mexico's colorful past.

Dorsey Mansion

> *Dorsey continued adding to his home and by 1886 the mansion had become a castle on the plains.*

by Laura Shubert

Northeast of Springer off of U.S. 56 lies a geological formation known as Point of Rocks. Here antelope and deer run across the plains, which shift from hues of gold-green to lavender as the day progresses. North past Point of Rocks are a few rocky foothills that nestle the Dorsey Mansion at their base.

The Dorsey Mansion is part log cabin and part Gothic Revival castle, built by U.S. Sen. Stephen W. Dorsey of Arkansas in the late-19th century. The mansion, once known for its spectacular parties and wide array of visitors, sat quiet and abandoned for many years. Today, it is open once again for visitors to enjoy year-round.

Dorsey, a carpetbag politician, railroad financier and sometimes less-than-reputable businessman, came to the wide-open spaces of Colfax County in 1877, having ac-

quired a large land grant known as the Uno de Gato. By 1878, Dorsey began construction on a log home he thought appropriate to a senator and up-and-coming cattle baron.

A visitor to the Dorsey Mansion in the early 1880s would have seen something quite different from the traditional adobe home that dotted the plains at the time. The well-constructed, 2-story structure was of hewn and oiled logs with a long veranda facing south. The interior was lavishly decorated, with a billiards room and museum for entertainment. A large man-made swimming pool boasted three center islands, one sporting a gazebo. Water to the pool was piped from a spring six miles away.

Dorsey continued adding to his home and by 1886 the mansion had become a castle on the plains. The new structure was a 2-story ma-

63

Above—Constructed originally as the home of Stephen W. Dorsey, the Dorsey Mansion also has functioned as a tuberculosis sanatorium, post office, general store, restaurant and, today, tourist attraction.

sonry house joined to the log home. The addition had a crenellated tower in which the likenesses of Dorsey, his wife, Helen, his brother John and a traditionally ugly gargoyle were carved from sandstone. The house had indoor plumbing and a carbide-gas lighting system. The grounds now boasted a smokehouse, fruit orchard, a rose garden that spelled out the name Helen Dorsey and a greenhouse, perhaps the first in New Mexico.

"It's not beautiful, but it is interesting," says Thomas J. Caperton, of New Mexico State Monuments and author of *Rogue! Being an Account of the Life and High Times of Stephen W. Dorsey*. No one really knows for sure who designed the mansion, although some speculate it might have been Fredrick Law Olmsted, with whom Dorsey was acquainted.

By 1892 Dorsey left New Mexico because of bad debts, charges of mail fraud and problems with business associates. Despite the cloud of notoriety, Dorsey did imprint some of his personal history on the state. In addition to the Dorsey Mansion, there is the nearby town of Clayton, named for Dorsey's son, and Mount Dora, 15 miles northwest of Clayton, named for Dorsey's sister-in-law.

From the time Dorsey left Colfax County until the early 1970s, the mansion was used as a tuberculosis sanatorium, post office, private residence and general store.

In 1972 the Dorsey Mansion was listed on the National Register of Historic Places and by 1976 it was a New Mexico state monument.

But due to a lack of funds, it was sold in 1987 to Roger W. Akers and Sandra Henning of California. The co-owners have opened the Dorsey

Mark Nohl

Mansion to the public year-round.

Today visitors to the Dorsey Mansion receive a guided tour of the building and grounds. Note the black-marble fireplace, the hand-carved, solid-cherrywood staircase and the ornate brass chandeliers, all part of the original Dorsey furnishings. The triangle dot motif repeated on much of the original woodwork—on doors, windows and even wardrobes and bedsteads—was Dorsey's cattle brand.

To get to the Dorsey Mansion, take Interstate 25 north to Springer then take U.S. 56 east for 25 miles, just past the first roadside rest area, before traveling the dirt road north for 12 miles.

The Dorsey Mansion is open to the public Friday through Tuesday, 10 a.m. to 4 p.m. by appointment only. Fees are charged for individual or group tours. If you are planning a trip to the Dorsey Man-sion, wear good walking shoes and call ahead for road conditions. For more information, call (505) 375-2222 or write to Dorsey Mansion, HCR 62, Box 42, Chico Route, Ratón, N.M. 87740. ✳

Above—*During its heyday, the Dorsey Mansion was one of the first structures on the northeastern plains to boast indoor plumbing, a gas-powered lighting system and a swimming pool.*

Mark Nohl

Cross-country skiers glide over a snowpacked trail at Enchanted Forest.

Enchanted Forest Cross-country Ski Area

Here at an elevation of 9,700 feet the snow is plentiful, the views are spectacular and the terrain is ideal for both track and backcountry skiing.

by Brian Shields

Dorothy reached over the glistening snow and grabbed a piece of German chocolate cake. "Are we having fun yet?" she asked, beaming in total satisfaction.

There were six of us partaking of the last of a variety of gourmet delights we had brought for lunch on our day tour of the Enchanted Forest Cross-country Ski Area. We spent the morning laughing, playing and skiing on some of the 18.6 miles of trails that spin their way like a spiker's web around the thick pine and fir knolls and aspenlined meadows on top of Bobcat Pass, three and one-half miles east of Red River.

Now we sat on our packs and leaned on our skis, which we had stuck in the snow to form a backrest. Satiated, we soaked up the sun that created rainbows on the freshly fallen snow and stared at the ridges of Wheeler Peak, Mount Walter and Old Mike. At more than 13,000 feet, they are among the highest mountains in New Mexico. The timberline, inviting in its winter mystery, called through the deafening silence of the wilderness.

As I started to doze off, I thought of what a great place John and Judy Miller chose for a Nordic ski center. Here at an elevation of 9,700 feet the snow is plentiful, the vews are spectacular and the terrain is ideal for both track and backcountry skiing. For instance, from where we sat dozing, we had a choice of skiing down a meadow on a well-packed trail that meanders, snakelike, around the untracked snow, or we could contour around the hill, making our own tracks through a glade of tall aspens then Telemark down any of a number of pitches that end up back

66

on the trail.

It is not by chance that the Millers have chosen this area. They have been involved with skiing in the Red River area since 1971 and have taught cross-country skiing and led tours throughout these mountains since 1979. They know the terrain well.

Since they opened Enchanted Forest, John and Judy have been joined by their daughter Ellen and son-in-law Geoff Goins, making the business a family affair. Ellen, who as a student at the University of New Mexico trained with the cross-country ski team, is now teaching at the area as well as clearing, packing, tracking and signing the trails. She also organizes numerous special events that range from serious clinics and races to the fun Easter Egg Scramble and the Just Desserts—Eat & Ski, when you "gorge out on delectable treats."

The 600-acre Enchanted Forest, which opened in 1986, is in its infancy, but the Millers have created a solid foundation upon which they are constantly making improvements. There currently are no facilities at the area to buy food, rent skis or get sunscreen. Those arrangements can be made at their store, Millers Crossing, or at other ski shops in Red River. Also lacking is adequate parking at the trailhead and easy access for anything but front-wheel- or four-wheel-drive vehicles. It is often necessary to park by the highway and walk or ski the quarter-mile to the trailhead.

The site offers the rank beginner easy access to the gentle meadows and spectacular vistas that are one-and-a-half miles from the present trailhead.

Red River is 38 miles northeast

Above—Dwarfed by the magnificent peaks of the Sangre de Cristo Mountains, this handful of cross-country skiers cut fresh tracks at the Enchanted Forest Cross-country Ski Area.

of Taos and 100 miles from Santa Fe. To reach the ski area, follow N.M. 38 into the Carson National Forest between Red River and Eagle Nest. Daily and season passes are available.

To get more information on the Enchanted Forest Cross-country Ski Area, write Box 521, Red River, N.M. 87558, or call (505) 754-2374.

Above—*Cross-country skiers plow through an untracked forest trail near Red River the morning after an abundant snowfall.*

Arnold Vigil

Rock cairns mark the start of the Gallinas Canyon Nature Trail.

Gallinas Canyon Nature Trail

Bird-watchers will spot a number of songbirds perched around the pools as butterflies glide across the path.

by Mark L. Taylor

You won't find it on the map handed out to visitors by the U.S. Fish and Wildlife Service folks at the Las Vegas National Wildlife Refuge Visitor Center. A person could drive around the area for a couple of weekends and never know the place exists. And when you finally do pull into the grassy parking area for the Gallinas Canyon Nature Trail, there's still room for doubt that you've actually found it.

The 8,750-acre federal wildlife refuge, a half-dozen miles southeast of Las Vegas, is a long-popular destination for migrating waterfowl and state bird-watchers. Every fall, Middle Marsh and Wigeon ponds fill with noisy, spiraling flocks of Arctic Circle ducks and geese.

During the winter the refuge is home to bald eagles that are often found sitting out on the ice of the frozen ponds or cutting lazy, circular flight paths across the empty, blue, prairie skies.

During the summer, bird-watchers can spot regal great blue herons, black-crowned night herons, red-winged blackbirds and flocks of ibis winging in low over the cattails.

Through it all, like some poor ignored stepsister, Gallinas Canyon sits off to the side of the wildlife refuge. But that's good news for the refuge visitor with a sense of adventure and a sturdy set of hiking boots.

Fish and Wildlife employees at the visitor center can provide directions to Gallinas Canyon and a free backcountry permit, which allows hikers to explore the trail only on Monday through Friday from 8:30 a.m. to 4:30 p.m.

No visitors are allowed into the

Arnold Vigil

Above—*A hike on the Gallinas Canyon Nature Trail takes visitors from the flat, plainslike terrain east of Las Vegas deep into rock-sided canyon lands decorated with colorful native foliage.*

canyon during wet weather and permits are not issued after 2:30 p.m.

Just beyond the parking lot's ragged fringe, hikers will spot about a dozen rock cairns staking out the trailhead. A couple of rock borderlines indicate the edges of the trail and snake off into the thick grass.

Following along, the path makes a sudden drop below the horizon of the surrounding swells of prairie. While you couldn't float it in an inner tube, the tiny Gallinas Creek, fed by spring runoff, triggers a startling flood of change in the narrow, rocky canyon.

Biologists describe such zones of unexpected, sudden and surprising change as microclimates. Hikers, artists and poets see such places as treasures to be enjoyed.

Here, in the narrow ribbon of Gallinas Canyon, the springwater

and cooler air that sink to such naturally low places have brought about diverse changes in the habitat.

But the most startling aspect of natural life along the canyon floor is the string of pools dammed up behind slabs of sandstone that have toppled from the canyon walls.

From kettle and bathtub size to that of a small backyard swimming pool, each catchment contains a supply of precious water and unique surprises.

Plump, old frogs spring from the muddy edges of the pools, gracefully pumping their long legs as they make for the cool refuge of deeper water.

A collection of spindly water bugs oar, stroke, paddle and hop across the glassy smooth pond surface. The grumpy croakings of the frogs ripple up and down the

70

Arnold Vigil

Arnold Vigil

length of this unexpected, lush and cool prairie oasis.

Bird-watchers will spot a number of songbirds perched around the pools as butterflies glide across the path. Overhead, along the lip of the canyon walls, one will find the ingenious inverted mud igloos of cliff swallows.

The chatter, click and buzz of insects provide a steady background noise and, most surely, a luscious diet of delectable, juicy bugs for bird and frog alike.

It is obvious—here in this hidden, moist retreat—that wildlife of all kinds are perfectly happy to spend their days in Gallinas Canyon.

Farther down, the canyon narrows and the path is lost to a scramble of tumbled boulders and even more pools. Eventually, the Gallinas River Canyon appears bordered by open, grassy flats.

Take a moment to sit on the cool grass, close your eyes and listen for a few long moments to the miracle of Gallinas Canyon—the precious miracle of free-flowing water.

To reach the Las Vegas National Wildlife Refuge Visitor Center, take N.M. 104 east of Las Vegas for two miles. Then turn south on N.M. 281 and follow the signs about four miles to the visitor center. 🔅

Above—A rock-lined path leads visitors on the designated route of the Gallinas Canyon Nature Trail. Above right—The rocky conditions of the canyon land make ideal seasonal habitat for several species of migrating birds.

Mark Nohl

A luminous Hermit's Peak overshadows the small northeastern village of Gallinas.

Hermit's Peak

> *Legend states that [the hermit] couldn't maneuver in his small mountainside cave without routinely cutting himself.*

by Arnold Vigil

Few natural landmarks equal the magical qualities of Hermit's Peak, a 10,263-foot-high mountain with dual granite precipices entrenched in the Pecos Wilderness about 18 miles northwest of Las Vegas, N.M.

Once known as *Cerro del Tecolote* (Owl Mountain), Hermit's Peak served as a landmark for west-bound travelers on the Santa Fe Trail. Its new name honors Juan María de Agostini, a reclusive holy man who gave up the advantages of Italian nobility in a worldly search for solitude and penance.

Agostini, known locally as *El Solitario* (The Loner) or *El Ermitaño* (The Hermit), found a cave on *Cerro del Tecolote* in the mid-1860s after walking on the Old Santa Fe Trail from Kansas. He walked alongside a wagon caravan led by Las Vegas merchant Don Manuel Romero. Agostini insisted on walk-ing despite numerous pleas by Romero that the holy man take a seat on one of the wagons.

Eventually living year-round on the peak, Agostini denied himself all luxuries, opting to sleep outside on the ground instead of on a bed when visiting nearby residents. Legend states that he couldn't ma-neuver in his small mountainside cave without routinely cutting himself. He refused all help from those concerned for his well-being.

Agostini, who is said to have healed the ill through herbal rem-edies and prayer, grew popular in the Las Vegas area. His pure life-style endeared him to *penitente* groups, who still practice their faith in his memory during pil-grimages to the top of the peak. Crosses fashioned from indige-nous trees are abundant on the mountaintop.

Residents of Gallinas would look

up to Hermit's Peak every night to see *El Ermitaño*'s campfire, a sign that the reclusive holy man was okay. Whenever the flame couldn't be seen, they would journey up the mountain to check on Agostini's welfare.

The hermit, however, quickly denounced his newfound popularity and left in 1867 to continue self-exile, which previously led him on foot through Europe, Central America, Mexico, Cuba and Canada. Ironically, Agostini met an unholy fate when he was stabbed in the back in 1869 near a cave he inhabited in the Organ Mountains. His body was found in a position indicating he might have been killed while praying.

The beauty of Hermit's Peak is complemented by the pristine Pecos Wilderness to the west and the lush Gallinas Valley to the east. A five-mile trail leads to the top

from El Porvenir Campground. A sign a few hundred yards to the right of a spring on the crest points the way to the hermit's cave.

Primitive camping is allowed on Hermit's Peak as well as the adjoining wilderness, where no motor vehicles are allowed. Other campgrounds are in the area, including Evergreen Valley and Camp Long.

Visitors who prefer not to hike the strenuous trail can arrange for horseback rides offered through two Gallinas Valley guest ranches—El Rito de San José, (505) 425-7027, and the Mountain Music Ranch, (505) 454-0565.

Picnics and overnight pack trips to the peak and the Pecos Wilderness, with llamas doing the grunt work, are offered through the Shining Star Ranch, (505) 425-1072.

Take N.M. 65 west from the Mills Avenue/Union Street intersection in Las Vegas to Gallinas Canyon.

Above—Once known as Cerro del Tecolote *(Owl Mountain), Hermit's Peak was renamed for Juan María de Agostini, or* El Ermitaño *as he was known to surrounding residents. Agostini gave up a life of nobility for religious solitude and penance.*

About 13 miles from the intersection is the right-hand turnoff to El Porvenir Campground, where a fee is charged for day/night use. Otherwise, free parking is available just outside the campground boundary.

A pass by the monumental Montezuma Castle, now occupied by the United World College of the American West, supplements the drive. The historic castle's roadside hot springs, a soothing site for sore hikers, are popular because there is no charge to take the plunge.

In addition to the wonder of Hermit's Peak, a journey farther west on N.M. 65 from the El Porvenir turnoff leads visitors to another road fork offering two excellent choices for sight-seeing or picnics.

A left-hand turn leads motorists on a graveled dirt road to Johnson Mesa, which offers excellent views of the Pecos Wilderness and Hermit's Peak. Many consider the road one of the most scenic in North America.

A right veer follows the Gallinas Creek to a trailhead at the end of the road, where about seven miles of the rugged Gallinas Creek Trail leads to the top of Elk Mountain. The 11,661-foot bald peak offers a breathtaking view of the Pecos Wilderness—13,000-foot-plus peaks and all.

For more information call the Forest Service, (505) 425-7472, or write the Las Vegas Chamber of Commerce, P.O. Box 148H, Las Vegas, N.M. 87701, (505) 425-8631. ❖

Above—The majesty of Hermit's Peak is still quite evident in this view of the landmark facing east from atop Elk Mountain. Johnson Mesa appears on the right while the beginnings of the Great Plains dominate the background.

Mark Nohl

La Cueva Mill on the David Salman ranch.

Mora Mills

> *La Cueva Mill's waterwheel still slowly turns, its creaks and groans appropriate for elderly machinery.*

by Larry E. Johnson

Stretching from the Sangre de Cristo Mountains into that vast ocean of land known as the Great Plains, the Mora River Valley is home to stock raising, Christmas tree farms, Territorial architecture and fiercely independent people. This valley, however, once could have been called the breadbasket of the Southwest.

Wheat and other grain crops have been grown since settlement began in the early 1800s. But it was the establishment of Fort Union in 1851 and the ever-increasing traffic on the Santa Fe Trail that greatly expanded the demand for flour and forage.

Mills, of course, were needed to produce flour, and two of the most productive out of the dozen or so in the area were St. Vrain's Stone Mill at Mora and La Cueva Rancho Mill a few miles south.

Today, both of these old mills are in need of repair, although the David Salman family, which owns La Cueva Mill, has done some preservation work on it.

St. Vrain's Stone Mill, built about 1864, is perhaps the more historic of the two, if only because of its prominent owner. Ceran St. Vrain led a colorful life as mountain man, partner in Bent's Old Fort in Colorado, Santa Fe Trail traveler and successful New Mexico merchant.

The stone mill was well-constructed for its day. It was supported by heavy wooden beams, many hewn by hand. A gambrel-style roof, with a steeper angle at the bottom than at the top, was made from corrugated metal and has stood the test of time well.

Stone blocks of varying sizes were used to construct its massive walls. These have weakened with age, and serious cracks threaten to bring down the beautiful, old

Above—Crumbling stone and adobe walls remind of a bygone era on La Cueva Rancho, where the wheels of commerce boomed to meet the demand for flour and forage along the Santa Fe Trail in the mid-1800s.

historic structure.

Behind the mill, a waterwheel sits sadly inactive, no longer attached to the drive shaft that turned its heavy stone grinding wheels. The flour it produced was coarse and gritty. But like other area mills, it could produce flour for about half the price of that shipped down the trail.

St. Vrain's Stone Mill is about one-quarter mile north of the intersection of N.M. 434 and 518, on the road to Coyote Creek State Park and Guadalupita. St. Vrain's home, a long adobe building now partially converted into a grocery store, is on the south side of the intersection in downtown Mora.

The extensive remains of the 33,000-acre La Cueva Rancho are found six miles south of Mora at the junction of N.M. 518 and 442. In addition to its picturesque mill, La Cueva's mercantile building,

storehouse, stone-walled corrals, cemetery, San Rafael Church ruin and the beautifully restored Vicente Romero House are nearby. The house, built in 1863, played host to such luminaries as Gen. William Tecumseh Sherman.

The mill, believed to be from the same era, is a large, two-story stone and adobe building with a corrugated iron roof like St. Vrain's. La Cueva Mill's waterwheel still slowly turns, its creaks and groans appropriate for an elderly piece of machinery. The water powering the wheel arrives via an excellent system of *acequias* (ditches) built by Romero to provide water for his fields. Verdant crops, including a flourishing raspberry operation, remain a part of La Cueva's aesthetic charm today.

The old mill is partially used for storage, but its windows, broken long ago, are now boarded up.

LA CUEVA MILL

THIS MILL WAS BUILT IN THE 1870'S BY VICENTE ROMERO.
IN 1851 HE ESTABLISHED THE LA CUEVA RANCH BY PURCHASING
LAND FROM SEVERAL GRANTEES OF THE MORA LAND GRANT WHICH
HAD BEEN CONCEDED BY GOVERNOR ALBINO PEREZ IN 1835.
ACCORDING TO LEGEND VICENTE ROMERO SLEPT IN CAVES WHILE
TENDING HIS SHEEP THUS THE NAME LA CUEVA.
FLOUR WAS GROUND AND ELECTRICITY WAS GENERATED BY THE
MILL UNTIL 1949.

PROPERTY OF WILLIAM SALMAN RANCH

Most of the machinery has been removed and its floors are in poor condition.

Since all of these structures are on private property, you should not trespass. With the exception of the Romero (Salman) House, they are easily viewed or photographed from either N.M. 518 or 442, however.

The old church ruin is one-half mile north of the mill on N.M. 442, across from the cemetery. From it, the house is partially visible through the trees to the southwest.

Both mills' commercial success ended with the coming of the railroad and subsequent abandonment of the Southwestern forts, including Fort Union in 1891. But St. Vrain's Stone Mill continued to operate until 1925 and La Cueva's until 1949. The nearby Cleveland Roller Mill was in use even later, handling special orders as recently as 1957. It now is the site of an annual arts and crafts fair.

These mills provide visitors with a nostalgic look back to the time when Mora County was one of New Mexico's most prosperous counties. ☀

Above—La Cueva Mill undoubtedly has seen better days, but thanks to the efforts of Mora's Salman family the site is being preserved as a historical treasure.

Mark Nohl

Ruins of a Spanish mission still dominate the skyline at Pecos National Monument.

Pecos National Monument

> ... *crumbled adobe walls suggest the majesty of the once-mighty village of Pecos.*

by Brandt Morgan

Pecos National Monument is a window to the past—a walk among the ruins of Pueblo, Spanish and Anglo people whose centuries of interaction have molded New Mexico.

The monument, about 25 miles east of Santa Fe, features museum displays of artifacts plus a meandering, 1.25-mile trail that snakes through acres of old ruins in an area once known as the Gateway to the Great Plains.

The best place to start your journey is the E.E. Fogelson Visitor Center, where you can view a film on the area's rich past and browse through a library and display rooms.

Displays include artifacts, outlining thousands of years of human history, with the mammoth, bison and camel hunters who first inhabited the area 12,000 years ago. Here you can view pots, arrowheads

and jewelry left by the Pueblo cultures from A.D. 800 to 1500; spurs, hoes, hoof cleaners and cactus pickers from Spanish frontier life through the 1700s; and even the hair curlers and tin coffee grinders of restless Americans heading west during the 1800s.

The area was declared a national monument in 1965 after 30 years as a state monument containing some 60 acres of ruins. That year, 300 more acres of rolling countryside were donated by E.E. "Buddy" and Greer Garson Fogelson. Garson-Fogelson recently sold the adjoining 18,000-acre Forked Lightning cattle ranch to the National Park Service, complete with peaceful hills and dramatic escarpments of the Pecos River Valley.

Pick up a trail guide at the visitor center and take the asphalt path that begins behind of the center. About 100 yards up the trail, you

will catch a glimpse of the ruins of a mission church built by the Spanish around 1625. Then you will wind around to the north, moving past vistas of meadows and pine-studded hills to the ancient walls that marked the boundaries of the north pueblo.

Soon you will come to a circular kiva, where you can take a ladder down into the dank, musty chamber that once served as the Indians' sacred place of meeting and ritual. Press a button on one of the vertical support beams and you'll hear the drumbeats and chanting voices of native people as they might have sounded hundreds of years ago.

Keeping your eyes peeled for hawks and eagles, wind up to the top of the hill, where big earthen mounds mark old trash heaps and crumbled adobe walls suggest the majesty of the once-mighty village of Pecos. During the 1400s, this vil-

lage included more than 600 rooms and rose 4 to 5 stories high.

As the trail veers west, take in the wide-open view, including a glimpse of Interstate 25 along the route once traveled by Indians, settlers, friars and soldiers between the Great Plains and the Colorado Plateau.

From here the trail snakes south to the remains of two Spanish-mission churches and courtyards. All that is left of the first is its stone foundation. Even the second, completed in 1717, is little more than an eroded shell with blue sky for a ceiling. But tasteful signs with etchings help visitors to mentally reconstruct these buildings and their adjacent, dark-halled *conventos*, and to understand the friars' powerful influence on the Pueblo peoples.

In August 1680, the Pecos people rebelled against the Spanish, burn-

Above—Some believe that Pecos Pueblo was the largest Pueblo Indian community in New Mexico when the Spanish first arrived in the 1500s. Spanish dominance dictated that the pueblo inhabitants abandon their native beliefs and turn to Christianity, symbolized by the mission church in the background.

ing and destroying the first mission. From the rubble, they built a new kiva to restore their own order. Though the Franciscans buried the kiva when they returned in 1692, it has been re-excavated and now sits in the middle of the *convento* as a symbol of the revolt.

Before returning to the visitor center, walk along the trail to the south pueblo mounds and ruins, another multistoried dwelling.

The Pecos people eventually abandoned the pueblo as a result of drought, famine and loss of trade. In 1838 the last of these hardy people walked to Jémez Pueblo, where their descendants still live today.

To get to Pecos National Monument, take Interstate 25 north from Albuquerque to Exit 307 (Rowe). Turn left on N.M. 63 and drive four miles to the park entrance. Expect to pay an entry fee.

There are several good picnic spots along the guided trail, one of them complete with benches and shelter. For overnight camping, call the U.S. Forest Service (505) 757-6121 for information on sites in the Pecos River Recreation Area off N.M. 63.

Above—*The thick adobe walls of the mission church at Pecos National Monument have withstood the test of time. The original church, however, wasn't so lucky as Pecos Indians destroyed the structure during the 1680 Pueblo Revolt. The present ruins originally were built after the Spanish reconquered the area more than a decade later.*

Mark Nohl

Brandon Nunn, in the white shorts, and his brother Will Nunn cliff jump at Ute Lake State Park.

Ute Lake State Park

The lake's many coves and crannies provide the right setting for recreation and privacy.

by Arnold Vigil

The rolling, semiarid hills of northeastern New Mexico must have seemed endless to Francisco Vázquez de Coronado and the members of his expedition.

They probably passed right by the area now occupied by Ute Lake State Park and the nearby community of Logan, leaving behind only the dust raised by the steps of their *caballos* (horses).

But even before conquistadores trudged through the area looking for gold and glory, it is believed Native Americans inhabited the rocky, dry sandy hills between A.D. 700 and 1200, subsisting on corn, beans and squash while hunting buffalo, antelope and deer.

These farmer/hunters were eventually driven out, however, by nomadic Indians who also wreaked havoc on later settlers until the U.S. Army began patrolling the area in the late 1800s.

The railroad brought an economic boost around the turn of the century and more settlers began to ranch and farm the land.

Today, man-made Ute Lake is a monumental paradox to the history and semiarid terrain, but a more-than-welcome oasis to vacationers, fishermen and recreation seekers. The lake was constructed in 1963 by the Interstate Streams Commission and its water capacity was increased in 1984.

According to park superintendent Rick Martin, the lake is mainly fed by Ute Creek with some water coming from the Canadian River overspill from nearby Conchas Lake State Park to the west. Martin says Ute Lake, the fourth-largest in New Mexico, is unique in that the water level fluctuates very little, unlike other lakes dependent on weather or used for irrigation.

81

Above—The marina and concessions area at Ute Lake State Park are equipped to handle demands of the thousands of water enthusiasts that visit the lake annually.

A ruling by the U.S. Supreme Court guarantees the water level at Ute Lake will remain relatively the same because of a long-standing lawsuit brought by the states of Oklahoma and Texas. Among other things, the court barred at least a dozen eastern New Mexico communities from obtaining municipal water from the reservoir—bad news for the cities but good news for lake users who can rely on consistent water levels.

The two neighboring states maintained that New Mexico drew too much water from the Canadian River when it enlarged the lake in 1984, contending a 1952 water-use agreement was violated. The Canadian River originates in New Mexico and flows through Texas and Oklahoma.

The lake's many coves and crannies provide the right setting for recreation and privacy. Along with

ideal conditions for black bass, walleye, carp, bluegill, catfish and shad fishing, the state park also welcomes water skiers, windsurfers, jet skiers, swimmers, divers, hikers and off-road enthusiasts.

Windy Point, a rocky area of the lake, is excellent for jumping and diving into the lake's warm waters. Teen-agers Will Nunn and his younger brother Brandon say they have been coming to the lake from their home in Tucson, Ariz., for more than 10 years.

"We look forward to coming here every year to visit our grandparents in Logan," Will says. "There's no place like this in Tucson where we can jump off rocks and swim."

Martin says the lake features two RV areas, each with 25 spaces and dumping stations. There are even two baseball fields, one used by residents of Logan for Little

League games.

Two comfort stations include rest room and shower facilities, Martin says, adding that there are numerous primitive and lakeside campsites, five concrete boat ramps and four docking areas. An on-lake concessionaire also offers overnight or yearly marina services as well as fishing and water-recreation goods.

Fees for park use are charged for individual vehicles per day, and overnight RV parking and use of primitive and developed campsites. Martin says there are also rates for yearly passes in addition to senior citizen and handicap discounts.

The friendly atmosphere of nearby Logan makes a stay at Ute Lake State Park one to remember. As one affable service station attendant puts it, "We better be friendly, especially when our live-lihood depends on the lake." Everyone, it seems, at the lake and in Logan is ready to be helpful—from the rangers at the park to the woman tending bar as well as the kid riding the bicycle.

The easiest way to get to Ute Lake is by taking U.S. 54 northeast 22 miles from Tucumcari, which is easily accessible east or west from Interstate 40.

More information can be obtained by calling the park at (505) 487-2284 or the Logan Chamber of Commerce at 487-2722. ❖

Above—There are many nooks and crannies within Ute Lake that offer the visitor much solitude. The area is ideal for a variety of water-related activities.

Geraint Smith

Thousands visit the DAV Vietnam Veterans National Memorial near Angel Fire.

DAV Vietnam Veterans National Memorial

The chapel is one of the few public buildings that always remains open.

by Emily Drabanski

To lose a child is one of life's greatest tragedies. When Victor Westphall heard of his son David's death in 1968 as a result of an enemy ambush in Vietnam, he was devastated.

But through his grief, he and his family chose to do something positive. They decided to have a chapel built that would be a remembrance of David and all those who served in Vietnam.

"It is in a very real sense not a war memorial, but a monument to peace," Westphall explains.

The beautiful chapel soars up from the Moreno Valley near Angel Fire like a dove of peace. Outside the wind blows steadily. Inside the chapel is a refuge for quiet reflection.

As the sun shines through a single glass shaft in the 50-foot structure, the visitor's thoughts return to another time in history.

Songs from the '60s play in the background. The tape recordings were made from David's record collection.

The visitor looks into the eyes of proud, young men in the 13 photographs that grace the chapel walls. David's photograph is always on display along with 12 others who lost their lives. It's a place for prayers, quiet reflection and often tears and hugs.

Throughout the year folks from around the country travel to the chapel. But it is particularly crowded on Veterans Day as many come to pay their respects to those who lost their lives in Vietnam.

The chapel, completed in 1971, was originally operated by the Westphall family but this proved to be a financial hardship. Fortunately, word of the chapel spread quickly.

In 1977, two officials of the Dis-

abled American Veterans stopped by on their way back from the Philmont Scout Ranch. "They had heard about the chapel because of national publicity," Westphall says. "They said when they got back they were going to send a flag because ours was tattered and worn. It was for a very good reason. We didn't have the funds to replace it.

"Several months later I got a phone call, but it wasn't about the flag, but $100,000. It was $10,000 a year for 10 years. After six years, they decided to set up a separate non-profit corporation called the DAV Vietnam Veterans National Memorial Inc. to assure its perpetuation." Westphall serves as the resident director.

Today, in addition to the chapel, the DAV operates a 6,000-square-foot visitor center. Large photographs of men and women who

fought in Vietnam depict the many roles they played in their military service. A book of more than 800 photos of those who lost their lives in Vietnam also is kept at the center. They are displayed on a rotating basis in the chapel. A videotape program tells the story of the chapel as well as the thoughts and reflections of many Vietnam veterans. Many children visit the center through programs in their schools.

Westphall is happy and proud that a national Vietnam memorial now sits in our nation's capital. But still thousands come to see the simple chapel in northern New Mexico that grew out of a family's grief and love.

"There's a grapevine among the veterans that just won't quit." Westphall says that some arrive in wheelchairs. And he relays the story of two men who served in the same company that found one an-

Above—The interior of the Vietnam Veterans National Memorial Visitor Center can have quite a sombering affect on those who visit. Many people who have seen the memorial testify that it somehow changed their opinion of the war.

Victor Westphall contemplates the consequences of war on steps inside the chapel he dedicated to his son David, who lost his life in Vietnam.

The smooth contours and free-flowing lines of the chapel produce a surreal, lasting emotional experience in memory of the hundreds of thousands of Americans who lost their lives in the Vietnam War.

other when they were visiting the chapel.

Many other aspects of the chapel make it unusual. "Originally, I decided there would be 13 photos on the walls, the cross would be 13 feet high and we would fly the original flag of our country with 13 stars. A year-and-a-half later I discovered there were 13 men in the company in which my son lost his life," Westphall says.

A granite picnic table is dedicated to veterans of all wars. Throughout the summer visitors can view brilliant masses of wildflowers. At last count, 42 varieties of wildflowers grow in the area. Some are native and others were planted.

The chapel is one of the few public buildings that always remains open. Westphall said once after he had locked it out of habit, he returned to find a plywood sign with a message scrawled in crayon, "Why did you lock me out when I needed to come in?" It's been left open ever since.

The chapel can be reached by some of the most scenic highways in northern New Mexico. Located via N.M. 434 and U.S. 64, it is a beautiful 28-mile drive from Taos, five miles northwest of Angel Fire and 10 miles south of Eagle Nest. For more information call (505) 377-6900.

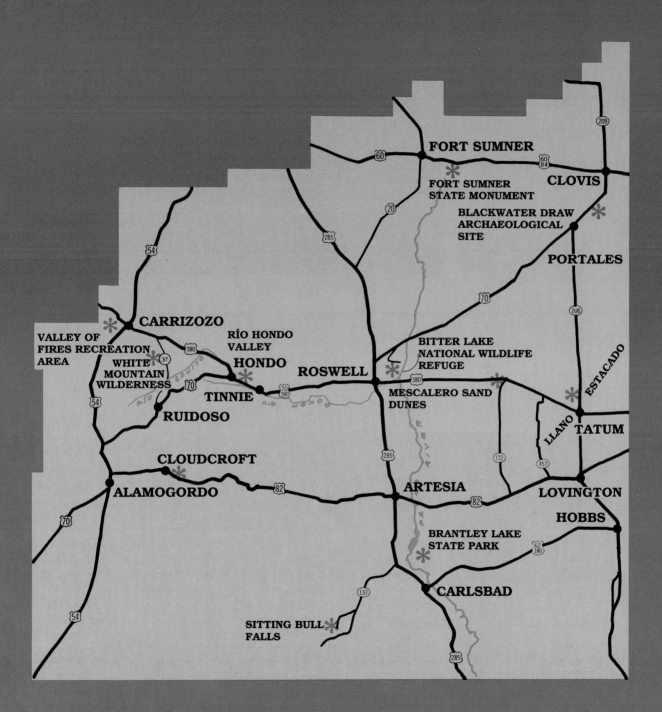

FORT SUMNER

FORT SUMNER
STATE MONUMENT

CLOVIS

BLACKWATER DRAW
ARCHAEOLOGICAL
SITE

PORTALES

CARRIZOZO

VALLEY OF
FIRES RECREATION
AREA

RÍO HONDO
VALLEY

HONDO

WHITE
MOUNTAIN
WILDERNESS

ROSWELL

BITTER LAKE
NATIONAL WILDLIFE
REFUGE

ESTACADO

TINNIE

MESCALERO SAND
DUNES

LLANO

TATUM

RUIDOSO

CLOUDCROFT

ALAMOGORDO

ARTESIA

LOVINGTON

HOBBS

BRANTLEY LAKE
STATE PARK

CARLSBAD

SITTING BULL
FALLS

Cathy Nelson

Snow geese take off from Bitter Lake National Wildlife Refuge, northeast of Roswell.

Bitter Lake National Wildlife Refuge

> *The best way to enjoy the refuge is to arrive either before sunrise . . . or just before sunset. . . .*

by Cathy Nelson

The sun has yet to rise on Bitter Lake National Wildlife Refuge, but already the chatter of snow geese can be heard dimly in the chill autumn air, while in the distant darkness white wings flash and dance.

Steam floats over the canals, whose smooth surfaces perfectly reflect the water-bound trees jutting up near the shoreline.

Then suddenly, as the first rays of daylight break the horizon over the red bluffs to the east, the lake explodes in a fury of flight.

Snow geese launch themselves with squadronlike precision, forming V-shaped lines in the brightening sky as they soar off in search of food.

Another day has come to this haven for migratory waterfowl, located along the Pecos River just 11 miles northeast of Roswell.

Established in 1937, the refuge's two land tracts total 23,310 acres and contain a water area of 750 surface acres when full.

The refuge takes its name from Bitter Lake, a small, alkaline playa lake fed by intermittent springs. Six man-made impoundments also attract a variety of nearly 300 feathered species.

Visitors to the southern tract, which is open from one hour before sunrise until one hour after sunset, will find it easy and fun to drive the 8½-mile, unpaved loop road around the lakes.

Numbered markers corresponding with information in leaflets available at the registration center help locate such stops as the snow goose overlook, from which 30,000 to 75,000 of the noisy birds can be seen during peak periods, to the marsh, which provides a habitat for rails, bitterns, egrets, herons and other wading birds.

Top—This flock of migratory fowl takes to the water during a lull in their travels south through Bitter Lake National Wildlife Refuge. ***Above****—These two mallards are considered drakes (males) because their feathers are more colorful than their female counterparts.*

Two other overlooks, at lakes No. 5 and 7, can be reached by driving up short inclines. They give the visitor a view of the surrounding area, including Capitán Mountain to the west.

The alert nature lover can recognize still more winged residents, such as ducks, Canada geese, roadrunners, quail, pheasants and hawks, while it's not unusual for a desert cottontail to dash across the road in front of an oncoming vehicle, especially after dusk.

While most snakes encountered on the refuge are harmless, both the prairie and Western diamondback rattlesnakes do occur, so caution should be exercised.

The best way to enjoy the refuge is to arrive either before sunrise, when the birds depart to forage in grain fields throughout the Pecos Valley, or just before sunset, when they return.

These are also the best times to photograph wildlife and scenery, since the light is not so harsh and the sun is not so hot.

For those planning a day trip, shaded picnic areas are available where you can have lunch and even a nap during the heat of the afternoon.

Fall is undoubtedly the best time to visit the refuge, when plant life along the shoreline often wears a coat of frost at sunrise. Mornings can be nippy, but the rest of the day usually features short-sleeve weather.

Winter also can be an interesting time to explore Bitter Lake, as the

Mark Nohl

Above—With squadronlike precision, a flock of southbound snow geese rise early to get a good jump on the search for food.

thousands of tracks crisscrossing in the snow attest to the presence of unseen creatures. The loop road, however, is sometimes closed due to snowdrifts.

Whatever the season, you'll experience more by parking your car and walking. Most of the refuge's 40,000 annual visitors make the mistake of cruising along at 25 or 30 mph, then wonder why they didn't see anything.

By just wandering, you're sure not only to see birds, but also to hear them. Standing atop one of the lookouts at twilight, you might be lucky enough to sense the presence of a flock of pelicans overhead, as strong wings beat ponderously in unison.

If you're not an early riser, sunset can be just as satisfying to visit the refuge. The late afternoons are golden and the western sky takes on a variety of hues, all reflected on the still water of the lakes.

When the lights of the city begin to blink in the distance, you might feel a sense of longing for an earlier time, when the horizon was unspoiled by telephone poles and lines, and great beasts roamed the landscape.

The refuge may be reached from east of Roswell, via Red Bridge Road off U.S. 380, or from north of the city, on East Pine Lodge Road, off U.S. 285 near the Roswell Mall. There are signs posted.

A small per-vehicle entrance fee is charged and season passes are available. Overnight camping is restricted to supervised youth groups, while hunting and fishing are permitted on certain portions of the refuge. Regulations are available at headquarters, (505) 622-6755.

A final bit of advice—don't forget to bring insect repellent. ◈

Mark Nohl

This view of a step trench at the site shows a bison bone and arrowheads made by early man.

Blackwater Draw Archaeological Site

> *It contains the earliest record of people in North America, including such archaeological materials as mammoth bones, Clovis points, scrapers, bone tools and so on.*

by Wendel Sloan

Looking at bones that are thousands of years old can give you a great sense of perspective. You can do just that by touring Eastern New Mexico University's Blackwater Draw archaeological site.

The Blackwater Draw Museum, located near Greyhound Stadium on U.S. 70 between Portales and Clovis, has been open since 1969 to show visitors examples of artifacts discovered at Blackwater Draw. But the site itself had been open to visitors only during sporadic tours. Thanks to an initial $75,000 grant from the state Legislature, however, ENMU recently opened the site to visitors on a regular basis.

Blackwater Draw, one of the most well-known and significant archaeological sites in North America, was discovered in 1932. It was the first site to document

man's existence in the New World, about 11,200 years ago. Artifacts found at the site indicate that the Paleo-Indians, the earliest known inhabitants of the continent, used spears to ambush huge mammoths watering at a large pond fed by the headwaters of the Brazos River. Camels, horses, bison, sabertooth tigers and dire wolves all once roamed the area.

Succeeding the Clovis culture were the Folsom hunter/gatherers, the Plano cultures, Archaic cultures and more recent Indian groups. Evidence indicates that the pond dried up about 7,000 years ago due to a widespread change in climate known as the Altithermal. Human occupation of the area, however, continued until about the time of Christ, as evidenced by the discoveries of camps associated with bison hunting and butchering.

Three structures were built to

Mark Nohl

Above—*The large jawbone of an ancient animal slain by prehistoric humans lies partially excavated at the Blackwater Draw archaeological site near Portales.*

make the site, located off of N.M. 467 between Portales and Cannon Air Force Base, more accessible to visitors: A caretaker's residence houses an archaeologist who lives on the site and helps provide security. The visitor center houses exhibits to help people understand what they will see at the site. The 50-by-100-foot overhang provides protection from the elements for both visitors and archaeological treasures. In conjunction with the overhang, an approximate 10-by-15-foot section of the south bank will be opened for new excavations so visitors can see artifacts as they are being discovered. A walkway was built from the visitor center to the overhang.

"Stabilization, interpretation and public access are the three objectives for the project," says Dr. John Montgomery, director of ENMU's Agency for Conservation Archaeology. "The real intent is to have a situation where people can know the site is here and schedule trips to see it." Montgomery says the site offers guided tours and an archaeologist available to answer questions.

"Blackwater Draw is probably the most important Paleo-Indian site in North America. It is the type-site for the Clovis culture, which is defined on the basis of discoveries there. It contains one of the earliest records of people in North America, including such archaeological materials as mammoth bones, Clovis points, scrapers, bone tools and so on. So when archaeologists speak about one of the oldest known cultures in North America, they are speaking about Blackwater Draw defining what we know about that culture.

"The site of today does not look like that of 11,200 years ago," says

92

Montgomery. "At that time, the site had abundant water. There were very cold streams and lakes, and lush greenery that was a very attractive habitat for mammoth and other animals. Because of the habitat, people utilized the area as a camping and kill site."

The project should enhance ENMU's status and become a boon to tourism for the entire area, Montgomery projects.

"We believe that the site is for everyone, not just archaeologists," Montgomery says. "It is a part of the heritage for all of New Mexico and, particularly, eastern New Mexico. It has vast potential for the entire region, as well as offering a unique aspect for our curriculum.

"The sky is the limit because of the unique nature of Blackwater Draw. It is amazing that such a relatively small investment can reap so many dividends in so many different ways."

Visitors can obtain more information by calling Montgomery at (505) 562-2254. Tours are led by arrangement from December through February. The rest of the year the site is open from 10 a.m. to 5 p.m. Tuesday through Saturday and from noon to 5 p.m. Sunday. Call (505) 356-5235 to book tours.

Above—*These animal remains still lie mostly in their natural state of burial at the Blackwater Draw site, which was first discovered by a highway crew in 1932.*

Lyndon Lee Watson

Brantley Lake replaced the century-old McMillan Dam, 10 miles upstream on the Pecos River.

Brantley Lake State Park

> *The original site of Seven Rivers, one of the wildest towns of the Old West, disappeared forever when Brantley Lake began to fill with water.*

by Marilyn Watson

Located about 12 miles north of Carlsbad and easily seen from U.S. 285, Brantley Dam is, in many ways, a marvel of engineering that also makes New Mexico's newest state park possible.

The dam's elegant neoclassic form rises like a soft-gray mirage out of teal blue water, lending an unexpected but welcome presence to a dry and desolate landscape.

About 140 feet high and 730 feet long, the center structure, or spillway, contains about 165,000 cubic yards of concrete, with a 300-foot opening that accommodates six massive, curved steel gates on hinges. The gates regulate the infrequent passage of flood waters, while two smaller hydraulic gates handle irrigation releases only.

The view from the top of Brantley is spectacular, with more than four miles of embankment that trace the course of an underlying tight sandstone formation. For safety reasons, the road over this area is closed to the general public.

To the south lies a county road that leads to recreational facilities on the east side of Brantley Lake.

Water from an outlet pool at the south base of the dam is continuously fed into an endangered-fish habitat nearby and channeled over to the Pecos River in varying amounts for seasonal irrigation.

A century-old dam, McMillan, 10 miles upstream from Brantley, was breached after construction of the new dam.

In 1964, McMillan was deemed unsafe, later paving the way for federal funding of Brantley through the Safety of Dams Program. In 1983, the first major work began on the project.

The total cost of about $140 million included new highway con-

struction, railroad track relocation, telephone and power-line rerouting and the installation of park recreational facilities.

The original site of Seven Rivers, one of the wildest towns of the Old West, disappeared forever when Brantley Lake began to fill with water.

Ironically, the old townsite now sleeps peacefully under a glistening blanket of water that will provide some of the best boating, fishing, waterskiing, windsurfing and camping opportunities in the state.

The state Department of Game and Fish stocks Brantley Lake on a regular basis with largemouth bass, catfish, walleye pike and, for forage, shad.

A plentiful supply of nutrients in the lake and a longer growing season should make good catches possible for fishermen.

Despite the seasonal extremes of a semiarid climate, numerous plants (creosote, mesquite, greasewood, cacti, grasses), animals (squirrels, raccoons, coyotes, bobcats, mule deer) and birds (owls, cranes, sparrows, gnatcatchers) are found in the Brantley area.

Some of these species exist in fragile microenvironments created through soil, water and elevation differences.

Although park facilities are still under construction, those on the west side of the lake—a parking area and boat ramp—are complete.

To reach this area, turn east off U.S. 285 about three miles north of the County Road 30/N.M. 137 junction, follow the road three-quarters of a mile to the new installations and join other enthusiasts in a variety of water sports and recreational activities.

Besides on-site provisions for the handicapped, the complex fea-

Above—The warmer climate of southeastern New Mexico makes for a longer growing season and provides fishermen at Brantley Lake great catch possibilities. The lake covers the area once occupied by the Wild West town of Seven Rivers.

Lyndon Lee Watson

Above—*About 165,000 cubic yards of concrete were used to complete the 140-foot-high and 730-foot-long spillway at Brantley Lake, New Mexico's latest man-made lake.*

tures a visitor center, full-service campground, comfort station with showers, dump station, day-use picnic area, boat ramp and courtesy dock, and an 80-space parking area.

For convenient entry to this area, drive north on County Road 34 from Carlsbad, or turn east off U.S. 285 onto County Road 30 at the N.M. 137 junction.

User fees initiated when the west-side facilities officially opened are moderate. Frequent park users, however, can save with the purchase of annual permits at any state park office or at the southeast regional headquarters in Carlsbad.

For more information call Brantley Lake State Park at (505) 457-2384. ⚜

Patricia Richardson

The Lodge at Cloudcroft has attracted visitors to the mountain community since the turn of the century. Fire destroyed the original 2-story log Lodge in 1909, but a larger version was rebuilt over the next two years and still stands as one of New Mexico's most picturesque landmarks.

Cloudcroft at Christmas

At night, crowds gather before a live Nativity scene, joining in choruses of favorite Christmas carols.

by Cal Stanke

Crisp, clear mountain air and an abundance of outdoor recreational opportunities attract visitors to the resort community of Cloudcroft throughout the year.

But December provides an especially good time to travel to the town, tucked away in the Sacramento Mountains 25 miles east of Alamogordo on U.S. 82.

Not only can you ski and go snowmobiling or inner tubing in the white-blanketed forests that surround Cloudcroft, but you also can partake of one of the state's most elaborate Christmas celebrations.

To reach Cloudcroft from Alamogordo, take U.S. 54 north for about two miles before turning east on U.S. 82. The winding journey will take you through five life zones, from Sonoran Desert in the Tularosa Basin to a Hudson Bay zone high up in the Sacramentos, towering as much as 9,700 feet above sea level.

Cloudcroft also can be reached from the east via U.S. 70 through Ruidoso. Turn south on N.M. 244 in the Mescalero Apache Indian Reservation.

Cloudcroft annually conducts a communitywide Christmas festival. Activities range from old-fashioned Christmas caroling to an unconventional pet parade. Some entries include snakes, goats, turkeys on leashes, goldfish in bowls decorated with wrapping paper and even invisible pets that only children can see.

Santa Claus leads the parade, only he doesn't ride in a reindeer-drawn sleigh. One year he touched down from Fort Bliss Military Reservation near El Paso, Texas, and cruised along U.S. 82 in an F-15.

Meanwhile, Mrs. Claus holds

97

court from her kitchen in Zenith Park behind the Cloudcroft Chamber of Commerce on U.S. 82. She hands out free cookies and hot chocolate, aided by elves in full costume.

A snow queen, nominated by students from Cloudcroft High School, is crowned and would-be artists compete in an ice sculpture contest, using 1½-foot ice cubes. Participants use everything from chisels and picks to rasps and saws to carve out their creations. Many of the sculptures reflect a Christmas theme, including Santa, sleds and toy-filled stockings.

At night, crowds gather before a live Nativity scene, joining in choruses of favorite Christmas carols. Camaraderie also is evident as people exchange hearty holiday greetings before a huge bonfire in Zenith Park.

Both businesses and homes are decked out in Christmas lights and wreaths.

Cloudcroft was established as a logging center after the El Paso & Northeastern Railroad opened a narrow-gauge line into the Sacramentos in 1899. An English settler gave it the name Cloudcroft, meaning a land where clouds can be seen in the crofts, or meadows.

Tourism always has been a Cloudcroft mainstay, particularly after the opening of The Lodge, a Bavarian-style resort, early this century. A sense of history pervades the rustic hotel, complete with a restaurant, saloon, roaring fireplace and beautiful resident-ghost Rebecca.

A skating rink, downhill ski facility and snowmobile rental shop are close to downtown Cloudcroft. The community even boasts a snow-covered, inner-tubing hill with a tow lift. ☼

Mark Nohl

A horse-drawn hearse joins a procession to the grave of Billy the Kid in Fort Sumner.

Fort Sumner State Monument

Fort Sumner residents bristle at the suggestion that the Kid eluded Garrett that fateful July night. . . .

by Jon Bowman

Janean Grissom stumbled across a gold mine when she saw the shiny coin half-buried in the sandy soil on her ranch east of Fort Sumner.

Grissom first thought she found a lucky penny. The coin, though, proved to be a worn Seated Liberty dime minted in 1881.

Excited by her discovery, Grissom explored the surrounding swale looking for more silver. She didn't find any more coins, but her good fortunes continued.

Amid the mesquite and scrub brush, she uncovered the rock foundation of what appeared to be an old shed or hut. Further investigation confirmed she had found the long-lost Stinking Springs rock house, where Sheriff Pat Garrett and a large posse captured Billy the Kid after a daylong gun battle on Dec. 23, 1880.

A state historic marker now stands near the entrance to the Grissom ranch in Taiban, about 14 miles east of Fort Sumner in eastern New Mexico. The weathered remains of the rock house may be viewed by the public on special occasions and by advance arrangements with Grissom.

Stinking Springs is but one of many Fort Sumner memorials to the most celebrated outlaw of the Old West. Behind Billy the Kid's Old Fort Sumner Museum, the bandit lies buried alongside two of his buddies, Charlie Bowdre and Tom O'Folliard.

Bowdre and O'Folliard died in the vicinity, Bowdre in the showdown at Stinking Springs. Billy was captured, jailed and sentenced to be hung, but he executed a daring escape in Lincoln.

With Garrett and his deputies hot on his trail, the Kid returned to Fort Sumner, where he had many

friends and favorite hideouts. His luck ran cold July 14, 1881, when Garrett gunned him down in the home of Pete Maxwell, nephew of land baron Lucien Maxwell.

Billy the Kid's tombstone reads, "The Boy Bandit King—He Died As He Had Lived." He never did kill 21 men, but that hasn't diminished his legend. Twice, souvenir seekers have stolen the outlaw's tombstone. Recovered each time, it now is strapped in iron shackles and protected within a cage.

Fort Sumner residents bristle at the suggestion that the Kid eluded Garrett that fateful July night, retreating to Mexico or roaming incognito across the West. The late Brushy Bill Roberts of Hico, Texas, and others who have claimed to be Billy are labeled as imposters here.

Chino Silva, whose grandfather was a pallbearer for Billy the Kid, says "We may have to start an-

other Lincoln County War" to fend off pretenders to the outlaw's throne.

Besides the Old Fort Sumner Museum and a separate Billy the Kid Museum, both full of photographs, newspapers and relics from the Wild West, visitors can take in Fort Sumner State Monument. About seven miles southeast of the town, the fort was built in 1862 to house Navajos and Apaches rounded up from their ancestral lands and marched to the reservation in the arduous 400-mile Long Walk. By 1868, the Indians returned home after many died of exposure, disease and starvation.

Little is left of the original fort and the Maxwell house has completely vanished, swept away during a flood of the Pecos River. There is a strong sense of history standing among the crumbling

Above—The disolved walls and foundation of the adobe Fort Sumner are faintly visible near Fort Sumner State Monument.

101

Above—The Fort Sumner State Monument Visitor Center sits in the middle of the area where the U.S. Army held captive many Navajos and Apaches rounded up on their ancestral lands in the 1860s.

adobe remains of the fort. A visitor center offers exhibits on Billy the Kid and the abortive incarceration of the Indians.

In San Jon, northeast of Fort Sumner, Old West buffs can watch the outdoor musical *Billy the Kid*, written by Clovis playwright Don McAlavy. It runs from mid-June through late August in the Caprock Amphitheatre.

June also is when Fort Sumner celebrates its annual Old Fort Days, featuring a windsurfing regatta at Lake Sumner, bicycle races, rodeos, dances, a simulated bank robbery, a parade and the Great American Cow Plop.

The highlight, though, is the Billy the Kid Tombstone Race, billed as the richest tombstone race in the world. Contestants, vying for a $1,000 purse, race over a 100-yard course, tossing heavy tombstones over hurdles along the way.

Fort Sumner and other southeastern towns host the inaugural edition of Billy the Kid/Pat Garrett Days, sponsored by the Billy the Kid Outlaw Gang. The celebration usually includes Billy the Kid, Pat Garrett, Deluvina Maxwell and Susan McSween look-alike contests, a Stinking Springs beef stew cookoff and a blanket horse race at Ruidoso Downs, when the event is in Ruidoso.

For information on Old Fort Days, contact the DeBaca County Chamber of Commerce at (505) 355-7705. The Billy the Kid Outlaw Gang is in Taiban at (505) 355-2555. The group of Old West buffs has members worldwide.

Fort Sumner straddles the intersection of U.S. 60-84 and N.M. 20. A trade center for surrounding farmers and ranchers, it lies about 50 miles southeast of Santa Rosa and 60 miles west of Clovis. ◈

Mark Nohl

The Llano Estacado, or Staked Plains, covers much of southeastern New Mexico. The plateau is among the westernmost extensions of the High Plains section of the Great Plains.

Llano Estacado

> *The Llano Estacado now is the breadbasket of New Mexico and produces more corn, hay, milo and peanuts than the rest of the state.*

by Wendel Sloan

If you use your imagination when driving across the Llano Estacado of eastern New Mexico, you can see and hear the past—replete with buffalo hunters, covered wagons and Billy the Kid. And just as the land has sparked conflicts between many factions—animals and their hunters, cowboys and Indians, outlaws and lawmen—so has the origin of the Llano Estacado name.

There are at least three theories about how the Llano Estacado, or Staked Plains, got its name. Robert Matheny, former president of Eastern New Mexico University and a professor of history explains: "One theory is that the Spanish explorer Francisco Vázquez de Coronado and his men, and others who came later, had to put stakes in the ground to tie their horses.

"Another interpretation is that the yucca plants across the prairie encouraged people to call it the Staked Plains. There is also the concept that stakes had to be driven in the ground to give people a sense of direction so they could find their way back."

Although there is some disagreement about what area constitutes the Llano Estacado, it generally encompasses eastern New Mexico north to Tucumcari and portions of West Texas. The Llano Estacado is a plateau that is part of the High Plains section of the Great Plains.

Although the present-day population didn't develop until the 1880s, based on the Homestead Act of 1862, man lived in the area long before then. Folsom Point or Clovis Point spearheads found at the Blackwater Draw archaeological site represent some of the oldest evidence of man's existence in the New World. The site, first occupied by man about 11,000 years

103

Above—*The silhouetted ruins of what once was a thriving homestead on the Llano Estacado reminds of what used to be in the flatland country.*

ago, was near a large pond fed by the headwaters of the Brazos River. The pond dried up about 7,000 years ago, but at the Blackwater Draw Museum near Portales, visitors can see evidence of wooly mammoth, camel, bison, saber-toothed tigers and dire wolves.

The Llano Estacado wasn't always a semiarid plain. "If you go back 11,500 years ago, we had spruce forests, pine trees, a number of large clear ponds, mammoth on the landscape, extinct bison and so on," says Phillip Shelley, associate professor of anthropology at ENMU. "That continued until about 9,000 years ago, then things started to dry out and shift to a grassland."

Thundering herds of buffalo roamed the Llano Estacado, but they were practically exterminated when more than a million hides were taken during the fall and win-

ter of 1877-78. The last recorded buffalo kill in New Mexico was at the now-dry Portales Spring.

While hunter/gatherers came and went through the Llano Estacado for thousands of years, the invention of the sodbusting plow and later discovery of the Ogallala aquifer, which made irrigation possible, signaled the beginning of a more permanent population. The Llano Estacado now is the breadbasket of New Mexico and produces more corn, hay, milo and peanuts than the rest of the state. A drive on the numerous farm-to-market roads, with modern tractors off to either side carving their way through the tall, gleaming greenery, confirms the breadbasket description.

One of the more striking natural attractions of the Llano Estacado is Railroad Mountain. Located southeast of Kenna on the White Lakes

Ranch Road north of Roswell, the small cliff looks like a train crossing the plains. About 100 feet high and a hundred yards wide, it runs for a mile or so and contains old petroglyphs with many geometric and stick figures. Another nearby attraction is the Bob Crosby Draw filled with gypsum, Pecos diamonds (quartz crystal) and killafish, a neon tropicallike species.

Museums throughout the region, including the Billy the Kid Museum in Fort Sumner, convey the area's rich past. Billy, who roamed all over the Llano Estacado during his brief life, was shot and killed by Sheriff Pat Garrett on July 14, 1881, in a bedroom of the Pete Maxwell home in Fort Sumner. The museum contains more than 60,000 relics of the Old West.

Although the Llano Estacado does not include the mountains, forests or lakes that other parts of the state boast, it has beauty of a rugged, subtle nature.

Above—These cute prairie dogs dwell on the flat, rocky terrain of the Llano Estacado. The area also is home to many other diverse species.

Mark Nohl

The Mescalero Sand Dunes provide opportunities for recreation as well as nature study.

Mescalero Sand Dunes

In non-vegetated areas, bare, light-tan dunes rise as high as 60 feet above the plains, still moving at an average speed of about a foot per year. . . .

by Anne Behl

The silence west of Mescalero Ridge is profound enough to give a modern traveler pause.

It must have given a 19th-century traveler chills, especially if he knew he was passing through Apache hunting grounds.

Forty miles east of Roswell along U.S. 380, in the shadow of a red outcropping known as Mescalero Ridge, tan sand dunes rise above the surrounding landscape. The area is part of the Caprock bordering southeastern New Mexico's Llano Estacado.

These are the Mescalero Sands, formed by the eroding power of wind, time and sparce vegetation. This surface of fine sand was left when the Permian Sea dried up 250 million years ago.

The Mescalero Sands extend for 60 miles, according to U.S. Bureau of Land Management (BLM) rec-

ords. Only the first few miles, visible from the highway and accessible via a caliche road, are open for public recreational use.

The Mescalero Ridge and the valley west of the sands were named for the Mescalero Apaches. The Apaches made their permanent home at the junction of the Sacramento and White mountains, west of the dunes. The reservation wasn't established until the 1870s, however, and for generations before that the Mescaleros wandered and hunted as far east as the Mescalero Ridge and as far north as Fort Sumner.

Deer and small animals still inhabit the area today, alongside domestic cattle grazing on BLM leases. The sands recreation area is about five miles west of the Lea-Chaves county line, a few miles west of a natural demarcation between the high, grassy plains east

of the Caprock and the rougher, brushier undulations that lead eventually to the Pecos River just east of Roswell.

The sands are divided into three areas: the Mathers Natural Area, the North Dune Recreation Area and the South Dune Area. The South Dunes have been designated an outstanding natural area, a unique desert habitat.

The Mescalero Sands are stabilized in some areas by almost-lush natural vegetation, including mesquite, chinnery, rabbitbrush and other hardy plants. The dunes and hummocks with the most growth show evidence of rabbits, lizards and birds, as well as many insects.

In non-vegetated areas, bare, light-tan dunes rise as high as 60 feet above the plains, still moving at an average speed of about a foot per year by prevailing southwest winds.

The access road from U.S. 380 is well maintained and easily driven by passenger cars. Facilities include two day-use parking areas with picnic tables, trash cans and a chemical toilet. Overnight parking is available, but the camping area has no water, electrical hookups or plumbing facilities.

The sands are 40 miles from Roswell and about three miles from the small Lea County ranching community of Caprock.

Spring and fall are probably the best times to visit the sands, although they should be accessible at any time of the year.

It's an uncrowded stop reachable from Roswell in less than an hour and from Hobbs in a little more than an hour.

For more information, contact the BLM Roswell Resource Area, Fifth and Richardson, (505) 624-1790. ⚜

Above—*The stunning lines and flowing curves of the Mescalero Sand Dunes in southeastern New Mexico remind of the Sahara Desert on the other side of the globe.* **Next page**—*The sparse vegetation on the Mescalero Sand Dunes, once part of the Permian Sea about 250 million years ago, wasn't enough to curtail eroding winds that shaped the surface into sand. Photo by Mark Nohl.*

Cathy Nelson

The Río Hondo Valley stands as a pastoral oasis in southeastern New Mexico.

Río Hondo Valley

. . . Hondo Valley is an emerald oasis, most resplendent from September to November when it is clothed in shades of green and gold, speckled with the humped shapes of black Angus cattle.

by Fiona Urquhart

The green, fertile valley of the Río Ruidoso and Río Hondo in southeastern New Mexico is one of the state's richest treasures and best-kept secrets.

Where the rivers descend from the Sacramento Mountains to parallel U.S. 70 from Ruidoso to Roswell, it ambles between arid, cholla-covered hills, creating an oasis of sumptuous color. In this lush valley of orchards and alfalfa lies a string of tiny towns—from San Patricio to Sunset—some so small they are gone before the traveler registers them. Yet this quiet, unassuming valley of little villages harbors a resident population of artists that rivals any in northern New Mexico.

San Patricio is the hub of this southerly artistic convergence. Set off from the highway in a dip of the valley, the village appears little more than a smattering of houses and a rustic church. Yet it boasts two art galleries and a polo field. Among its population of 250 are several members of one of the country's most famous artistic family.

Henriette Wyeth, daughter of the eminent painter N.C. Wyeth, came to San Patricio in the early 40s with her husband, New Mexico painter Peter Hurd. Well into her 80s, Henriette still paints in the studio of the 200-year-old adobe ranch home she shared with Hurd until his death. Two of their children, also artists, live nearby.

The Hurds' son Michael opened a gallery to exhibit work by the San Patricio family. On its walls are paintings by Michael Hurd, his parents and work by his sister, Carol, and her husband, Peter Rogers. Behind the elegant adobe building, 20 species of trees flourish in the luxuriant grounds.

Above—*The Hondo Valley, relatively un-discovered in terms of population and tourist numbers, boasts the same classic New Mexican architecture found in other parts of the state.*

Hurd built his gallery, which he named La Rinconada, on a corner of the village polo field. The San Patricio Polo Club, which, Hurd says, has none of the "snobby overtones of polo in Palm Beach," consists of 30 playing members, making it the largest club in the U.S. Polo Association's Border Circuit.

When his parents settled in San Patricio, Hurd says, they drew other artists to the area like a magnet. One of those was Peter Hurd's friend John Meigs, a fellow painter and avid collector of art and antiques. Meigs bought a three-room, adobe railroad cottage across the river from the Hurds. As his collection expanded, so did his house, until Meigs had added another 18 rooms. Fort Meigs, with its fluttering U.S. and New Mexico flags, dominates the village. Meigs was in his mid-70s when he decided to sell off his huge collection of paint-

ings, furniture, ceramics, quilts, tapestries, books and sundry paraphernalia. Several rooms in Fort Meigs have been turned over to gallery space and are open to the public seven days a week.

Four miles east of San Patricio, in the village of Hondo, where the Río Ruidoso and Río Boníto converge to make the Río Hondo, the traveler might catch a glimpse of a newly finished work by another of the state's most prominent artists.

On occasion, outside the old converted schoolhouse that functions as a studio, one of Luís Jimenez's brightly painted, monumental Fiberglas figures hangs suspended from a chain over the loading dock, ready to be hoisted onto a truck.

A tall bell tower and weather vane herald the visitor's approach to the village of Tinnie. Back in 1882 the long, Territorial-era build-

110

ing beneath the tower was the Tinnie Mercantile Co., a general store and post office. Today the Tinnie Silver Dollar is an ornate, Victorian-style restaurant furnished by John Meigs with authentic antiques. Its many rooms are adorned with carved mirrors, gaslights, stained glass windows and oil paintings (one room is dedicated to the work of Peter Hurd). Outside on the veranda diners also feast on a superb view of the Hondo Valley.

The quiet hamlets of Picacho and Sunset are the final settlements along the highway before the Río Hondo diverges a few miles to the south. The people of these five communities cherish the verdant habitat and beneficent bounty they share with the river. In the Upper Chihuahuan Desert, where there are few streams, the Hondo Valley is an emerald oasis, most resplen-

dent from September to November when it is clothed in shades of green and gold, speckled with the humped shapes of black Angus cattle.

Beneath the sapphire sky of a New Mexico fall, cottonwoods and Lombardy poplars saturate the valley with a heady infusion of gold. Above the paler gold of the earth, Stellar's jays flit between the peach-tinted branches of a tamarisk. And along the length of the valley, numerous fruit stands display the rich soil's sweetly fragrant yield—cherries, apples, pears, plums and peaches, chile, squash, peanuts and honey—a profusion of nature's bounty in New Mexico's valley of artists. ❋

Above—Beautiful scenery such as this autumn setting in the Hondo Valley have made the southeastern area a popular haven for artists and other creative people.

Peter Greene

Sitting Bull Falls cascades about 100 feet in the Guadalupe Mountains west of Carlsbad.

Sitting Bull Falls

The rocky streambed is worn smooth by centuries of running water.

by Lois Purvis

Water spilling from the top of a steep cliff in the Guadalupe Mountains forms Sitting Bull Falls. It plunges downward and creates a cool climate on the floor of a high-walled triangular canyon in Lincoln National Forest.

The falls must be reached on foot. Trails are well-defined and accessible, and a series of concrete steps and walkways take the visitor on the final lap to the falls, curving around a bend to the right of a picnic area.

Legend has it that ranchers pursued Chief Sitting Bull and his followers to the waterfall after they stole horses and cattle in 1881. But former state historian Myra Ellen Jenkins debunks that Sitting Bull was in Canada in 1881 and probably never visited New Mexico.

More likely, the waterfall got its name from Bill Jones, an early set-tler and renowned storyteller who was among a group that found the site in 1881. Jones told so many tall tales that some folks felt his account of the waterfall was just plain bull. Thus, a name was born.

Many who have never visited the waterfall are familiar with it. Sitting Bull Falls was featured during the 1950s in the Hollywood movie *King Solomon's Mines*, substituting for an African locale.

Sitting Bull Falls attracts good-sized crowds because it is the state's most accessible waterfall by foot. The round-trip walk is less than a quarter-mile. Leaving the parking area at the entrance to the recreation area, the visitor is directed by a wooden sign that says: "Sitting Bull Falls 150 yards."

The trail leads past picnic shelters that are open on all sides but have roofs for protection from sun and rain. Each of about 10 shelters

W. P. Fleming

contains two tables with benches and a charcoal grill.

Native plants flank the trail, including a large prickly pear cactus in various stages of blossoming that attracts several diligent bees.

The traditional vegetation of the semiarid mountains gives way to trees of desert willow, walnut, piñon and juniper along the stream flowing from the falls. The rocky streambed is worn smooth by centuries of running water.

Near the walkway that begins the final lap before the falls, not yet visible but clearly heard, a squirrel scurries across the base of the first step. Earlier, several of the bushy-tailed animals helped themselves to food that picnickers left out on a table in a nearby rock shelter.

Approaching the falls in the small canyon, protected on three sides by steep cliff walls, is as refreshing as entering an air-conditioned room from midday desert heat. The cooler temperatures and presence of water raises the humidity, creating ripe conditions for plentiful vegetation.

During late spring, summer and early fall, swimmers and waders crowd into pools at the base of the falls. The collected water is deep enough to allow an adult to swim, and children frolic along the edges of rock-lined pools.

Visitors have discovered another cooling treat for the more adventurous—climbing rocks on the steep face of the cliff where water cascades downward. The source of the supply is a spring on the flat surface of the bluff above. The water falls 100 feet in three streams from the top, spreading into glistening sheets and separating into smaller streams in the plunge downward.

A forest sign asks, "Where does the water go? This question puzzles many people," the marker continues. "The water disappears first into the gravelly bottom. It then runs into the cracks in the base rock or bedrock of these mountains. The water may reappear from springs farther down the canyon or run through underground rivers into the groundwater supply along the Pecos Valley.

"As the slightly acid water seeps through the rock, it dissolves the limestone and caves like Carlsbad Caverns are formed. In the Guadalupe Mountains over a hundred such caves are known. Probably," the sign observes, "many more are awaiting discovery."

Sitting Bull Falls is about 50 miles west of Carlsbad in the Guadalupe Ranger District of Lincoln National Forest. Travel north from Carlsbad on U.S. 285 and turn left on N.M. 137 and continue west until the road forks. At that point, turn right on County Road 409 and continue eight miles.

The road leads directly into the Sitting Bull Falls parking area through a gate open 6 a.m. to 10 p.m. daily from April through November. Overnight camping is prohibited, and the site is closed to the public from December through March.

Rest rooms and a drinking fountain are available. Paths and all facilities are well-maintained. No fee is charged for parking or use of the area. ✤

Previous page—Located in the remote Guadalupe Mountains, Sitting Bull Falls is popularly believed to have been named after the famous Indian chief, who was followed to the site by a group of ranchers irate that the chief and a band of his followers stole livestock from a ranch in Seven Rivers in 1881. At least one historian disputes this account, claiming that Sitting Bull was in Canada at the time of the alleged rustling.

Mark Nohl

One mile west of Carrizozo off U.S. 380, Valley of Fires Recreation Area contains one of the nation's youngest and best preserved lava flows. The river of volcanic rock extends about 44 miles, ranging in width from half a mile to more than five miles.

Valley of Fires Recreation Area

> *. . . cholla, solitary sotol and gray-green saltbrush seem to grow from the blackness of the lava, but windblown soil . . . is the real source of nutrients.*

by Darrell J. Pehr

The sun, setting into red-rimmed clouds above a darkened horizon of ragged peaks, throws beams of brightness across the rippled black mass of the lava flows at Valley of Fires Recreation Area.

The lava flows, a 44-mile stretch of cracked black *malpais* (badland), erupt across the desert valley near Carrizozo like a burnt pepperoni pizza long forgotten in Paul Bunyan's oven.

Motionless ebony waves swell 10 and 20 feet into the breezy blue sky. Like a new-moon tide, the lava gushed into the valley 15 centuries ago, finding its way up the lowest elevations, split only by uplifted hills and ridges.

The *malpais* is dark, unmoving and without the molten heat that once gave it life.

But a surge of life did come to Valley of Fires soon after the out-pouring of lava ceased from Little Black Peak, a volcano a dozen miles north of the park.

Dull-green prickly pear the size of dinner plates sprout maroon fruit and red-tan needles on the side of one mound of lava. Nearby, cholla, solitary sotol and gray-green saltbrush seem to grow from the blackness of the lava, but wind-blown soil, caught in the folds of the black basaltic rock, is the real source of nutrients.

Junipers twist in a wooden mimic of the lava's swirls. Gramma grass and the spiny algerita, too, bring life-giving green to the blackness where hundreds of animals also live. Mule deer, howling coyote and tiny scaled quail make the lava bed their home. Lizards, perhaps the most easily and frequently observed residents, dash across the lava at a frantic rate.

A self-paced interpretive trail

Above—New Mexico's volcanic past is never so apparent as in Valley of Fires Recreation Area, where ebony lava waves 10 and 20 feet high spewed from a volcano (now Little Black Peak) 12 miles north of the area about 1,500 years ago.

loops out across the *malpais* from the park's sandstone-island base, a hill 30 feet higher than the lava that surrounds it. Coded red markers at places of interest along the trail are explained in a park brochure. Plant and animal life, as well as details on characteristics of the lava flow, are described. The 45-minute walk follows the black rock's twists and curls across part of the area's 462 acres. The entire flow, which ends up in the south along the northern end of the White Sands, covers 172 square miles. At 1,500 years old, the flow is one of the youngest and best preserved in the lower 48 states.

East of the trail are Valley of Fire's picnic, camping and playground areas. Twenty covered picnic tables encircle the peak of the sandstone island. Each also can be used as a pull-through camping spot and many are furnished with electricity.

Camping fees at each developed site are for a maximum of seven nights, primitive sites and electrical hookups. Those rates include an entrance fee per vehicle. Busload rates are slightly more.

A large, covered picnic shelter, containing eight picnic tables, a drinking fountain and a barbecue grill, is available by reservation.

The park gates are usually open from 7 a.m. to sunset. A self-service pay station at the entrance asks visitors for "honest support so that we may better serve you." Fees are used for daily operation and maintenance of the park. The area is patrolled and citations are issued to visitors who fail to honor the pay station.

Brochures are available at an information center and plans are in motion for a visitor center. Reservations and information are avail-

Mark Nohl

able by calling (505) 624-1790, or writing Valley of Fires, P.O. Box 871, Carrizozo, N.M. 88301.

Valley of Fires is two and one-half hours from Albuquerque via Interstate 25 south and U.S. 380 east. It is three miles west of Carrizozo on U.S. 380. Carrizozo offers the traveler many motels, a handful of restaurants and a cluster of service stations and convenience stores, says Betty Howell, owner of Four Winds Motel and president of the Carrizozo Chamber of Commerce. She reports visitors to the area from Switzerland, Germany, France, England and Americans from as far away as Maine have come to see the desert's "river of fire."

"It's really amazing how many come," she says, pointing out that 5 to 10 percent of her guests come to visit Valley of Fires.

Even the residents of Carrizozo find themselves drawn back every so often to experience again the drama of Valley of Fires. Howell finds June is one of her favorite times to visit, when cacti bloom at the park.

The blooms, some red and some yellow, are as unpredictable as the shadows cast across the black rocks' ripples by a setting sun. As Howell describes Valley of Fires Recreation Area, "It's always different." ⚜

Above—*Although not able to sustain plant or animal life on its own, vegetation exists in Valley of Fires because of topsoil blown onto the site by wind. These typical Southwestern plants attest to the phenomenon.*

117

Dianne deLeon-Stallings

A hiker relaxes on an isolated boulder in one of the meadows along the 22-mile Crest Trail.

White Mountain Wilderness

In late summer, visitors might be buzzed by hummingbirds hurrying to harvest wildflower nectar or by swarms of ladybugs. . . .

by Dianne deLeon-Stallings

When the mercury bubbles each summer, thousands flee the sweltering heat for the cool breezes and alpine scenery of the White Mountain Wilderness about 50 miles northeast of Alamogordo.

With nearly 125 miles of trails, the wilderness ranges in elevation from 6,500 feet to about 11,500 feet and offers recreation for hikers who are interested in a leisurely daytime excursion or who are determined to experience nature at its most challenging.

The abrupt changes in elevation translate to equally dramatic changes in plant life. On a single trail, high-desert scrub trees, creosote, yucca and prickly pear cacti give way to willows and pine along creek beds, and then to mixed conifers in high-mountain meadows.

Camping in the wilderness is limited to backpacking, but in the Lincoln National Forest that adjoins portions of the tract, campgrounds and throw-down areas provide overnight bases accessible by vehicles. Only foot travel is allowed inside the wilderness.

Although summer is the most popular season, the wilderness is open year-round. Aspen, oak and maple color swatches of brilliant yellow, orange and red on the hillsides during the fall, and wildflowers create a cornucopia of colors in the spring.

Even in winter, when 10,255-foot-high Elk Point is under 6 feet of snow, campgrounds and trails at lower elevations might present comfortable outdoor opportunities.

No matter when you visit, layered clothing is the best bet. While campers at Three Rivers between Carrizozo and Alamogordo off

118

U.S. 54 might be suffering from temperatures of more than 100 degrees, the thermometer barely hits 70 in the higher mountains. Plan for afternoon showers July through August and gusty spring winds.

Established by Congress in 1933 as a primitive area, the 48,000-acre wilderness was incorporated into the National Wilderness System in 1964. The C-shaped range follows the ridge of the mountains, encasing the site of what was once Bonito City. The settlement was dismantled in 1935 when a reservoir was built, creating Bonito Lake, whose water was needed to feed the steam locomotives of the Southern Pacific Railroad. Old apple orchards and rusty mining equipment remain as reminders of the past.

The U.S. Forest Service is committed to maintaining the feeling of remoteness while guaranteeing users convenient access to the trails, says Forester Peg Crim, who handles recreation and wilderness supervision.

Nine trailheads, many near designated camping areas, mark the entrances to the system of trails. Threading its way for 22 miles along the spine of the mountains is Crest Trail, the major route that ties together dozens of other hiking offshoots running along streams and down canyons. Crim says a favorite hike is Rodamaker Trail, which follows a path from Bonito Lake to emerge in an upland meadow studded with flowering plants. Short-horned lizards scurry across the meadow floor, fixing intruders with a stony stare.

From the forestry fire tower at Monjeau Peak, the east-west chain of the Capitán Mountains sprawls below. In late summer, visitors might be buzzed by hummingbirds

Above—The White Mountain Wilderness in southeastern New Mexico offers excellent retreat from the urban madness and summer heat.

hurrying to harvest wildflower nectar or by swarms of ladybugs on their annual pilgrimage to the rocky outcrops around the peak.

Crim has been stationed at White Mountain for more than three years and the view from Crest Trail still moves her, she says.

"It always amazes me," Crim says. "From the top, you can see the gypsum dunes of White Sands National Monument and the lava beds of Valley of Fires, and all of it is backed by the San Andres Mountains."

When backpacking, check with the Smokey Bear Ranger District office at Ruidoso and purchase a waterproof map with trails and freshwater springs marked.

Campgrounds are not luxurious. Most lack running water. Three Rivers, the only wilderness access from the west, is one of two camp-

grounds with corrals for those who plan to tackle the trails on horse-back.

South Fork Campground, near Bonito Lake, is the only fee area. Extras include running water and modern sanitary facilities. Access to most campgrounds is by forest roads off N.M. 37 northwest of Ruidoso.

To contact the ranger office, call (505) 257-4095 or write 901 Mechem Drive, Ruidoso, N.M. 88345.

Above—Many abrupt changes in elevation within the White Wilderness mean a diversity of plant life. The area ranges in elevation from about 6,500 feet to heights of about 11,500 feet.

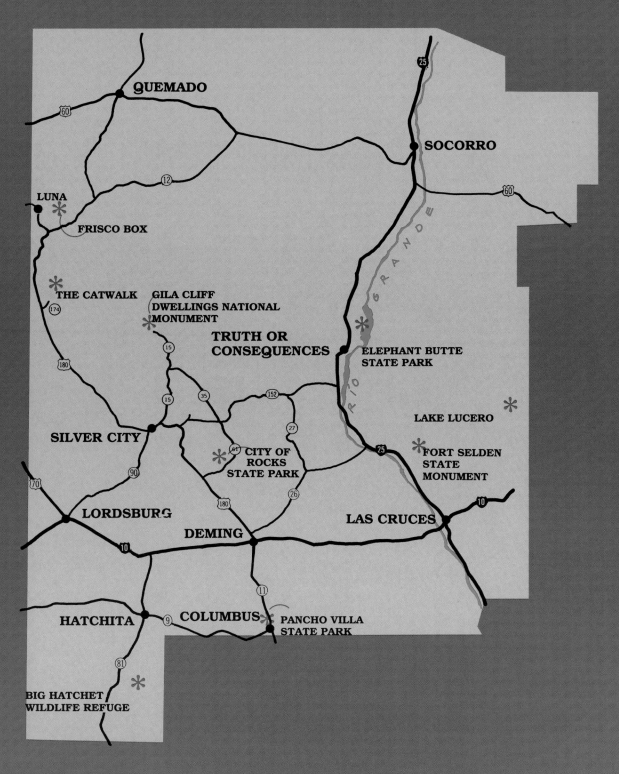

QUEMADO

SOCORRO

LUNA

FRISCO BOX

THE CATWALK

GILA CLIFF
DWELLINGS NATIONAL
MONUMENT

TRUTH OR
CONSEQUENCES

ELEPHANT BUTTE
STATE PARK

LAKE LUCERO

SILVER CITY

CITY OF
ROCKS
STATE PARK

FORT SELDEN
STATE
MONUMENT

LORDSBURG

DEMING

LAS CRUCES

HATCHITA

COLUMBUS

PANCHO VILLA
STATE PARK

BIG HATCHET
WILDLIFE REFUGE

Albert D. Manchester

The remoteness of the Big Hatchet Mountains is obvious in this view from the west.

Big Hatchet Wildlife Refuge

> *This is New Mexico before the Sunbelt was discovered. The last half of the 20th century seems to have passed by without stopping.*

by Albert D. Manchester

You don't find the Big Hatchet Wildlife Refuge by accident, not unless you just happen to be driving along N.M. 81 between Hachita and Antelope Wells in the southwestern corner of the state. Antelope Wells, by the way, is the southernmost—and most remote—customs and immigration post on the border. Berrendo (Spanish for antelope) is the Mexican equivalent of Antelope Wells and lies just across the international cattle guard. Carlos Johnson, whose father was a Canadian, has been the Mexican immigration officer at Berrendo since 1950. Johnson reports that only four or five vehicles will pass through on any given day.

So almost nobody just happens to drive by the Big Hatchet Wildlife Refuge. However, if you're hankering for a taste of the Old West of 50 years ago, you've come to the right country. Narrow paved highways give way to narrower graveled roads as you approach the border. This is open range; cattle roam freely across the roads. You'll find no hamburger stands, no drive-up windows. You will find a few small grocery stores, a couple of cafes and three gas stations, one each at Hachita, Rodeo and Ánimas.

Solitude. You learn about the sound of silence. A soaring hawk—or a cautious coyote who studies you over his shoulder as he trots away—may be the only movement in the wide land. This is New Mexico before the Sunbelt was discovered. The last half of the 20th century seems to have passed by without stopping.

Big Hatchet Wildlife Refuge lies just to the east of N.M. 81. The refuge occupies 105,000 acres of the Big Hatchet Mountains, a north-

122

west-southeast trending range that is rather like an island in its corner of the Sonoran Desert. The highest peak, Big Hatchet, rises to 8,366 feet. These are steep, rugged mountains, irregularly folded and striated, pale pink on the peaks, reddish brown or gray on the lower elevations. Juniper and piñon are the dominant vegetation on the higher slopes, while creosote, mesquite and a mix of desert shrubs cover the lower slopes.

The wildlife refuge was established in 1926 for the propagation of the desert bighorn sheep (*Ovis canadensis mexicana*), a shy, sensitive, endangered creature that finds humans to be impossible neighbors. Well, if the bighorns need solitude, the Big Hatchets are as good a place as any. At last count 105 of the sheep were seen on the peaks, up from a low of only 12 in 1979 after most of the original

herd perished in a drought. The present herd has grown from transplants north of Lordsburg (a Department of Game and Fish trailer seen in the area was called a "ewe haul"). Apart from an exciting variety of reptiles, other wildlife possibly seen in the refuge are the desert mule deer, ring-tailed cat, fox, mountain lion, badger and javalina.

Although hardly as dangerous as when Apaches led by Cochise and Mangas Coloradas raided at will, this is still rugged, desolate terrain. You'll find little water, no designated camping sites, almost no roads . . . or what the more urban motorist might think of as a road. This is four-wheel-drive, high-clearance country where you might need your own water, extra gasoline and two spares. And remember, there are no resident rangers on duty should something

Above—*A dilapidating church in Hatchita, a small southwestern community in New Mexico's Bootheel country, manages to represent that region's sparse population.*

123

Albert D. Manchester

Right—*The Big Hatchet Mountains were named for the rock, adzelike protrusion jutting from the range on the left.*

go awry out there in the hills and canyons.

To enter the refuge, you are dependent on the goodwill of ranchers who own the land across which you'll have to drive. One rancher holds the key to a gate; at another place, several miles from the highway, you have to drive through a corral. Although they are kind and courteous—even charming—you get the impression that the ranchers, like the bighorn, enjoy their solitude.

And the Department of Game and Fish requests that the backcountry of the refuge not be visited from February to May, the spring lambing period for bighorns. Intrusions during this period could be disastrous to the herd. Faced with too much pressure, the desert bighorns have been known to abandon their habitat.

Back in the hills you will find beautiful, isolated areas like Thompson and Sheridan canyons. But always keep in mind that you are not in a park. The refuge belongs to the animals it was set aside to protect. This is wild, quiet, clean desert country. We must leave it as we find it. ⁜

124

Andrew Gulliford

The Catwalk offers spectacular views of Whitewater Canyon.

The Catwalk

In the 1880s, on the lam and dogged by Pinkertons, Butch Cassidy and the Wild Bunch hid out in the narrow canyon.

by Peter Russell and Sharman Apt Russell

In the arid Southwest it is commonly said that water flows uphill to money. But Whitewater Creek, a small tributary of the San Francisco River flows decidedly downhill.

It drains the highest country in southwestern New Mexico—37 square miles of 10,000-foot peaks—and some of the wettest. Where the creek breaks through the mountains into the San Francisco Valley, the water funnels through a gorge of sheer rock about 200 feet wide and 100 feet deep. When it rains, it roars. Above the gorge, giant boulders jam sections of the deep canyon and the water sluices between them, loud and splendidly white.

Through this gorge and for about a mile up the canyon winds the Catwalk, a national recreation trail and one of New Mexico's more unusual day hikes. Along traces of a 19th-century pipeline, a steel walkway hangs over Whitewater Creek, carrying visitors through the gorge to the canyon above. Twenty feet below, the creek flows quietly—most of the time. On the left, slightly higher than the Catwalk, is a sign that marks the high water level of the 1971 flood. About 5 feet above that mark, snagged on an anchor bolt, is some river debris from the flood of 1983.

Beyond the gorge, the trail continues as an easy path 50 or so feet above the water. Parts of an older trail, the occasional abutments of a washed-out bridge and a few stout, timbered supports are visible below. Here and there a sycamore anchors itself among the boulders. Alders and sometimes a grove of Gambel oak give shade along the stream, while the canyon walls, rising 1,400 feet, gradually open to more light and to grass.

Peter Russell

Above—Giant boulders and gushing water make Whitewater Canyon a challenging and excellent place for hiking enthusiasts. Desperados and marauding Apaches used the narrow canyon as a hideout in the 1800s. **Opposite**—*The Catwalk offers an exciting but safe journey through steep canyon walls over Whitewater Creek.*

does enter its story. In the 1880s, on the lam and dogged by Pinkertons, Butch Cassidy and the Wild Bunch hid out in the narrow canyon. So did Apaches, who were still raiding with Gerónimo and Nana. Prospectors risked—and some lost—their lives for the gold and silver strikes that became the Confidence, the Bluebird, the Blackbird and the Redbird claims.

In 1889, a mill to service these claims was built below the gorge, where Whitewater Creek finally emerges onto some flatland. In 1893, a 4-inch pipeline was laid through the gorge and along the canyon's west side for three miles to provide water for the mill's electric generator and for the 200 or so inhabitants of Graham, the town that grew up beside the mill. Another larger pipeline was laid in 1893. These pipelines needed frequent maintenance, and the workmen who repaired the damages had to walk along the suspended pipes that were referred to as the catwalk. Today portions of the pipelines are still visible.

The mill was only moderately successful and it closed in 1913. Just a few stone walls of the mill remain, built into the hillside above the parking lot at the trailhead. Graham is altogether gone. In the 1930s, Civilian Conservation Corps workers rebuilt the Catwalk as a recreational attraction and in 1961 the U.S. Forest Service built the steel walkway that visitors use today.

The trail begins below the ruins of the old mill, in a large grove of sycamores that shade picnic tables where families can sit and watch their children play along the usually quiet stream. Fishermen often work the deeper pools above the gorge, as do water ouzels and occasional kingfishers. Netleaf oak, a generally rare tree, is common along the canyon sides, attracting botanists. Backpackers hike up the canyon and into the Gila Wilderness, which begins about a mile beyond the suspension bridge.

To reach the Catwalk Trail, drive to Glenwood on U.S. 180, 60 miles north from Silver City or 40 miles south from Reserve. In Glenwood, turn east on N.M. 174, pass the state fish hatchery and continue for five miles. The road dead-ends at the Catwalk. ❧

Occasionally the trail drops to the level of the water and in one place a steep metal staircase descends to an especially fine pool. Frequent handrailings along the exposed side of the trail—especially where it is cut into the rock side of the canyon—preserve the feeling of a catwalk.

The trail crosses the creek three times on progressively more interesting bridges: a wooden bridge, a steel bridge that was flown in two sections into the canyon by helicopter and a swinging suspension bridge that ends, with the trail, on a ledge. Below, white water crashes among boulders.

The water in Whitewater Creek doesn't flow uphill, but money

126

Mark Nohl

Towering boulders at the southwestern New Mexico park resemble the monoliths at Stonehenge.

City of Rocks State Park

> *Photographers contort to catch the towers of stone against a turquoise sky or the miracle of a scrub tree rising out of rock.*

by Sharman Apt Russell

It catches you by surprise. Unseen from the state highway, down a two-mile spur of blacktop, the City of Rocks State Park rises suddenly from a vast yellow plain of waving grama grass. The columnar, pastel stones make an uneven and disheveled skyline. Some tower as high as 50 feet. Others hunker to the earth like brooding trolls. In the interior of "the city," rocks meld and merge to form arches, curvaceous streets and dark alleyways. Off to the side, isolated on the yellow plain, small groups of standing stone look like gentle giants—caught in a gossipy conversation.

The effect is weird and fantastical. This is a city of dreams, a city of particular delight to children and to adults who can still imagine and think as children do. This is the place to play games of enchantment, to clamber over warm boulders like a darting lizard, to run and hide and scheme in a geological playground that is relatively small but perfectly scaled.

At 5,000 feet, on the edge of the high Chihuahuan Desert, the park's 40 acres of jumbled rock are a product of volcanic activity followed by erosion.

Some 33 million years ago, volcanoes erupted in this area and spewed out fiery particles of rock. When the particles settled, they fused to form a layer that geologists call "kneeling nun rhyolite tuff." (This odd term comes from a local landmark, some miles to the north, in which an eroded pillar of volcanic tuff seems to kneel submissively just below a mountain peak.)

As the solid layer cooled, it cracked and splintered. Rain, snow, frost, sun and blasts of desert sand further eroded the mate-

Honey mesquite blossoms in the desert sun as brooding boulders at the City of Rocks congregate in the background.

129

Above—Volcanic in origin and formed by wind and erosion, the rocks resemble mythical creatures to the imaginative. Evidence found under the sand at the site suggests ancient Indians once used the giant stones as shelter from the natural elements.

rial into their modern, compelling shapes. The tedious and seemingly invisible process of erosion can be seen today as scales of rock slip away from a tower's fractured surface, leaving a smooth, rounded hump of stone underneath.

The vertical inclines of this state park attract rock climbers and boulder enthusiasts. Hikers can wander up to the high rimrock that overlooks the city or walk the road leading to a panoramic view of the Mimbres Valley and fang of Cooke's Peak. Photographers contort to catch the towers of stone against a turquoise sky or the miracle of a scrub tree rising out of rock. Desert lovers enjoy the cultivated botanical garden with its neatly labeled species of cacti, both exotic and native.

All visitors appreciate the park's arrangement of camping and picnic sites. Several dozen spots with tables and fireplaces are concealed among the labyrinthian metropolis. Firewood, however, is not available. A 1.5-mile dirt road

circles the main portion of eroded tuff, so that motorists and RV campers can drive slowly around the park before making their selection. These camping areas are nestled carefully amid the trees and rock walls and are rarely within sight of each other. Healthy Emory oaks shade many of the tables and the nearby stone blocks out noise and creates a sense of privacy. Faucets and rest rooms placed along the dirt road are all easily accessible. One restroom boasts the camping comfort of solar-heated water. Near the front entrance is a playground with swings and slides.

With little water in the area, prehistoric Indians probably did not make these rocks a permanent home. There are, however, Mimbreño ruins in the surrounding area. And within the tuff itself are holes where seeds and nuts were ground over many years. In 1852, the explorer John Bartlett passed near the City of Rocks and missed it completely. Instead he was

greatly impressed by a few isolated stone pillars that he named the "Giants of the Mimbres." A hundred years later, the City of Rocks State Park was created.

Where human visitors come and go, wild animals make their home. Pack rats and chipmunks scurry over the rocks; ravens, hawks and owls hunt from above. Antelope, deer and coyote can be seen in the surrounding desert.

The animals, of course, live here for free. Others must pay. There are daily fees per vehicle, busloads and overnight camping. A visit is well worth the price.

The City of Rocks State Park is 27 miles northwest of Deming and 31 miles southeast of Silver City. Branching from U.S. 180, N.M. 61 runs past the entrance to the park and on up the rural Mimbres Valley with its tree-lined river, apple orchards and irrigated fields. The road continues north to the Gila National Forest and on toward the Gila Cliff Dwellings National Monument. ✺

Mark Nohl

A butte resembling an elephant gives New Mexico's largest lake its name.

Elephant Butte State Park

> *On Memorial Day weekend the park becomes the state's second largest city with a population of about 90,000.*

by Bill Dyroff

Just before first light on almost any day in June, a few vehicles trailing boats will back down the main launch ramp at Elephant Butte Lake State Park in south-central New Mexico.

Efficiency seems to be the rule as silhouette figures quietly launch boats for an early start at fishing. Their craft glide softly over calm water past the courtesy dock and nearby marina.

Once beyond the protected no-wake area, motors are turned up for a run to Elephant Butte's remote upper lake. Dawn breaks over the Fra Cristóbal Mountains that parallel the lake on the east side. As boats speed up, the rush of cool, early morning air is certain to awaken any sleepy rider.

Boaters pass between Rattlesnake and Horse islands and turn north. On good years the boaters could be off to a 40- to 45-mile trip.

With low water-level years the trip might be reduced to 30 miles. That still represents plenty of water in New Mexico's largest lake.

The early reveille anglers are only the vanguard. Soon, camps along the shoreline show the glow of morning fires. As the rising sun warms the lake and winds pick up, the surface comes alive with colorful sailboards and small sailing craft moving out to relatively sheltered areas. Larger sailboats, some with strikingly beautiful sails, glide past prominent landmarks—rising out of the water just north of the dam, the butte that resembles an elephant and for which the lake is named; Kettle Top Butte, a chopped-off volcanic cone on the east side about six miles above the dam; and farther to the north, the stark lava look of the Black Bluffs.

The Butte is an impoundment on the Río Grande built by the Bureau

131

Mark Nohl

Above—Ships ahoy! In addition to water skiers, fishermen and windsailers, Elephant Butte Lake offers excellent winds for sailboating, a sport not readily identified with the semiarid Southwest.

of Reclamation and dedicated in 1916. It was constructed to store irrigation water and once was the largest man-made lake in the world, according to the bureau.

Elephant Butte Lake has a long hourglass shape with irregular edges. It consists of a main body extending about 14 miles north of the dam and an upper lake whose size depends on how much water has been impounded. The two are connected by a constricted four-mile stretch of the Río Grande known as the Narrows.

At capacity, Elephant Butte Lake offers nearly 37,000 surface acres and 250 miles of shoreline. Dependent on snow runoff in the Río Grande watershed and reduced annually by the draw for irrigation, the surface acreage varies widely.

Located between Albuquerque and El Paso, Elephant Butte attracts about 1.75 million visitors a

year. On Memorial Day weekend the park becomes the state's second largest city with a population of about 90,000.

Elephant Butte is accessible from Interstate 25. The state park generally runs the length of the lake. Standard park fees for day use and camping apply throughout.

For first-time visitors, a stop at the park headquarters and visitor center is advisable. From I-25, take Exit 83 and follow signs for about five miles. Signs along the route will also direct visitors to Rock Canyon Marina, Elephant Butte Resort Marina, the dam and the Damsite Recreation Area.

Just beyond the visitor center is Ridge Road with areas overlooking the lake designed to support picnicking and camping, including sites with electricity. It also leads to a children's playground, Lyons Beach and a special section of

campsites that can be reserved by calling the park office.

The dam is 1,162 feet long and 301 feet high. In 1939, power-generating capability was added. It is activated when irrigation water is released. Bureau personnel will conduct tours of the power plant and galleries inside the dam. Simply check in at the office below the dam on weekdays before 3 p.m.

There are many entry points along the 40- to 45-mile length of the state park to lakeside sites with such colorful names as Jet Boat Cove, Catfish Camp and Three Sisters. A popular remote site is the Rock House area, near the middle of the Narrows. Take Exit 92 off I-25, follow the frontage road on the west side north about two miles, then go east under I-25 and follow signs to Rock House. The area has limited facilities, but provides excellent access for fishing the Nar-

rows and upper lake.

Boat camping has become popular. There is a potential problem, however, with trespassing on private land. Campers should seek guidance at the park office.

The Butte has an excellent reputation for black bass and white bass fishing. Recently, striped bass have been in the limelight with average stripers running 15 to 20 pounds with some in the 45- to 50-pound range. A list of authorized guides is available at the park office.

Recreational vehicle parks are at Damsite, east of the dam, and on the west side of the lake near Monticello Point. Damsite has a marina, cabins, restaurant and lounge.

For more information, contact the state park staff, (505) 744-5421.
✺

Above—Marina facilities at the Butte make the area particularly inviting for overnight boaters. The beautiful New Mexico sky also provides a fringe benefit.

Frank D. Thayer Jr.

Ranger Joe Guzman inspects a stabilized wall at Fort Selden.

Fort Selden State Monument

> *Tourists who tread the tree-lined walkways at Fort Selden are actually walking 2 feet above the ground where cavalry and infantrymen rode and marched. . . .*

by Frank D. Thayer Jr.

To walk the paths of Fort Selden today is to sense the isolation and tedium of a frontier New Mexico soldier's life, yet many who visit this state monument probably are not aware that one of the toughest battles of Fort Selden is being waged even as they stroll its paths.

At the fort, where a 4-year-old Douglas MacArthur first learned to ride, where black and white soldiers alike were stationed over a period of 26 years to protect the swelling numbers of settlers from New Mexico's Indians and sometimes from each other, today's "soldiers" are fighting to preserve the ruins from sinking back into the earth from which the adobe walls were first fashioned in 1865.

From the center of the quadrangle, where an exact replica of the original flagpole stands, it is easy to imagine the sun blinking messages from the mirror of a heliograph on Robledo Mountain just across the meandering Río Grande and to remember that one of the most aggravating depredations of the Apaches was that of cutting the rope with which the troops crossed the river.

Tom Caperton, director of state monuments, emphasizes that twice as many soldiers were killed in intramural squabbles in the nearby town of Leasburg than died from Indian arrows during those early years.

Tourists who tread the tree-lined walkways at Fort Selden are actually walking 2 feet above the ground where cavalry and infantrymen rode and marched, and that is what brought the scientists to southern New Mexico to save this dissolving resource. Most of the added soil on the floor of Fort Selden has come from the walls.

The state started an $84,000 preservation study recognizing the importance of preserving historic monuments such as Fort Selden. In the northeast corner of the fort, once a garbage dump, adobe walls were constructed in 1984. These walls were capped and coated with a wide variety of materials.

It was obvious to Caperton that not only would these test walls help the state save Fort Selden, but the findings would benefit adobe homeowners and builders the world over.

The world is paying close attention to Fort Selden because the test wall project is monitored by sophisticated scientific instrumentation that can tell how the great enemies of adobe—capillary seepage and old-fashioned rain—affect various brick structures, caps and coatings. The manager of Fort Selden, Ranger Joe Guzman, does a precise continuing photo study of the walls so that Caperton's office can apply what it has learned to saving historic New Mexico buildings.

The test walls at the fort have been patched, braced with "steel sandwiches" and, more lately, the remaining walls have been topped with adobe mud. Visitors might see red tape protruding from the tops of some walls; when this tape is exposed, the rangers know they must add more mud to keep rain from washing away original bricks. Many of the original bricks at Fort Selden contain bits of pottery from Indian pots, broken to bring strength to Army adobes.

Scientists such as those from the Getty Conservation Institute in California believe the adobe problem "will be solved," Caperton says.

Fort Selden easily is reached

Above—The crumbling adobe walls at Fort Selden show their years. Initially constructed in 1865, historians are working hard to preserve the remnants of this U.S. Army fort named after Col. Henry R. Selden of the 1st New Mexico Infantry and one-time captain of the 5th U.S. Infantry.

Above—The orderly ruins of Fort Selden suggest of the regimentation employed by the U.S. Army in the 1800s. The fort was built to protect settlers from Apache Indians, but soldiers saw little action of this type during its 25-year existence.

from Interstate 25 or U.S. 85. The I-25 exit is the same as that for Leasburg Dam State Park, 13 miles north of Las Cruces and 17 miles south of the Rincon exit. Visitors will find a museum exhibit of fort artifacts and styles to begin and end the tour of the fort itself. Signs mark the parade ground, officers' and enlisted men's quarters, and all the other important areas still defined by foundations and ragged walls that turn salmon pink with sunset while the wind makes whispering noises in the grass.

With the black silhouette of Robledo Mountain defining the end of the day, walk back to the museum beside the old corrals and imagine the vague images of blue-uniformed troopers preparing for evening formation in a New Mexico that is not so distant in time as you might have thought.

Peter Russell

Towering rocks signal the beginnings of Frisco Box.

Frisco Box

In places its walls rise a thousand feet and the sky shuts down to a narrow swatch of blue.

by Sharman Apt Russell

I f the perfect day hike combines beauty, drama and moderate physical activity, then an excursion to the Frisco Box offers perfection. A scenic drive leads you to the trailhead. The walk is pleasantly level and the three-mile trek climaxes in a startling box canyon the width of a large living room. Through this room flows the San Francisco River. Craggy rock walls rise above the stream bed that in many places also is the canyon bottom. Amid this harsh geology, cottonwoods and alders have found a foothold, adding further lushness to the green of Virginia creeper, grapevine, willow and wild rose.

This is a world mysteriously hidden and exquisitely scaled: a world of rock, water and intense, shifting patches of light and shadow. Here, adventurers can start their canyoneering, a new term for the wading, swimming, leaping and bouldering involved in squeezing through a narrow canyon.

To find the Frisco Box, you must first find the town of Luna in Catron County. Near the Arizona border, Luna is on U.S. 180, about 100 miles west of Socorro. Your first stop should be the Luna Ranger District where you can check for local fire and river conditions. In the monsoon months from July through early September, you do not want to be scaling the walls of the box canyon with a flash flood raging beneath.

From the ranger station, you'll turn right at the church and drive four miles down Forest Road 19, left on Forest Road 210 and another 8.4 miles. This area is part of a private ranch and you will stop twice to open and close gates. The meadows are broad and beautiful against wooded hills unfolding be-

137

low blue-gray cliffs and lavender mountains.

Up to now, the dirt road is smooth enough for any car. The last mile or so, however, has more of what you have been expecting—sudden bumps, dips and angry looking rocks placed directly in front of your tire. Just before the San Francisco River is a steep and rocky hill. You'll want to park at the top or in the open area before.

A trail starts at the bottom of the hill and follows the river eastward. In about a half-mile, the Frisco Divide Trail intersects and heads south. Continue along the riverbanks, crossing here and there, and possibly get your feet wet as the water curves in a shallow valley of grass and shrubbery. In another mile, you'll see signs of trickling springs along the west bank. Fifty feet up is a natural hot spring with a concrete pool and wooden bench. Sometimes a sign announces the spring. Sometimes not. But you are sure to find it if you keep on the right side and remember that the spring is above the river.

After an hour's walk from your car—about three miles—the trail enters the box. The approach is oblique. One moment you are in the bright sunshine. Then you are poised before the dark and deliciously cool entrance. From the cliffs a yucca shoots up its flowering stalk, and the scarlet flash of claret cup peeks from a ledge.

The rest of the hike will involve some swimming or thigh-deep wading. How deep or how many pools there are depends on the stream's flow and on the canyon itself as it narrows and widens. Birds flicker overhead. Lizards and frogs jump from your footsteps. The sound of water grows suddenly harsh as the river speeds down an incline over pebbles and stone; then the music will soften to indicate depth. Yellow flowers bloom in the cracks along the cliff and long grasses brush against your bare legs.

About a half-mile down the box is a jumble of rocks, as though part of the wall tumbled down. One boulder is the size of a small cottage and the passage here requires minimal mountaineering. Many visitors stop here, perch and stare at the primal scene below: the cacophony of rock and the play of a

Above—*The San Francisco River flows out of the Frisco Box. The river winds between the San Francisco and Mogollón ranges in a southerly direction along the Continental Divide, before it veers west into Arizona and empties into the Gila River.*

river in the dry Southwest.

The Frisco Box continues for about a mile and a half. In places its walls rise a thousand feet and the sky shuts down to a narrow swatch of blue. Those who plan ahead can have a car waiting where the box opens onto Forest Road 41 near Reserve. Be sure and check the condition of that road with the ranger district.

Other walkers will be content to retrace their steps, three miles back along the river. If you have time, stop at the hot springs, plug in the cement pool and take a warm bath. On the way out, the odds are good that you will see a few ducks or a great blue heron, its strong wings flapping, its posture serene even in flight.

Opposite—*Although not for everyone, the journey through Frisco Canyon makes simple hiking an adventure. Besides cool mountain water, a hot spring along the way is sure to delight.*

Mark Nohl

A branch of the Mogollón Indians inhabited the cave dwellings at Gila until mysteriously disappearing about 600 years ago. The national monument not only contains the ruins but also is gateway into the Gila Wilderness, the first designated wilderness area in the nation.

Gila Cliff Dwellings National Monument

The acoustics of the caves and respect for a mysterious past invite quiet conversation and more thought than talk.

by M.H. Salmon

On the edge of the Gila Wilderness, nearly 200 feet above a canyon creek, the remnants of Indian cliff dwellings give us a view of the lives of a people who simply disappeared into history.

Known as cliff dwellers, these Pueblo Indians began to inhabit caves along the west fork of the Gila River about A.D. 1280. In less than 100 years, they vanished from the region, leaving their dwellings, some tools, exquisite art and a mystery.

Gila Cliff Dwellings National Monument lies at the end of N.M. 15, a twisting paved road and a scenic adventure in itself, 44 miles north of Silver City. At the footbridge over the west fork of the Gila River, pick up a pamphlet guide. This is the starting point for a one-mile hike that takes the visitor, first, up a beautiful canyon.

Cottonwood, willow, pine, piñon and oak keep one in the shade during the first half of the hike, while the traveler repeatedly crosses a slender creek in the canyon. From rock and wood benches in the canyon, you can look up at the dwellings in the caves, far above in a south-facing cliff.

A half-mile into the hike, the climb begins. It is not severe and, again, nature's own rocks and trees provide rest stops. The trail loops around and now runs parallel nearly 200 feet above the creek, as the first cliff house appears on the left.

These Pueblo Indians were part of the Mogollón culture. They chose their homes wisely. The natural caves reach 20 to 30 feet back into the bluffs, high enough that even a modern 6-footer can stand up in them. In front of the caves, a natural porch provides a walkway from one cave to the next. Facing south, the mouth of each cave provides shade. From these lofty homes, the cliff dwellers had a beautiful view of the world and natural protection from human enemies.

Many of the rooms within the caves are still standing. They were largely of adobe bricks built around timbers that formed the walls, windows and doors. In most cases, the roof of each room was simply the overhang of the cave. Seven caves are in the side of the cliff; five retain dwellings that contained about 40 rooms.

In some rooms, depressions in the floor indicate where grain was ground—likely a pueblo kitchen. Other rooms are quite large and were probably meeting places or communal rooms. Large smudge marks blacken the roofs of the caves, indicating where fires were built.

Archaeologists have determined that the cliff dwellers were partly farmers, and sometimes hunters and gatherers. Crops included corn, squash, beans and tobacco. They grew these plants along streams and on the mesas above the canyon. They also were skilled hunters who left finely crafted obsidian arrowheads. Then as now, the Mogollón Mountains offered a tremendous variety of small and large game as well as oak and piñon nuts and other food suitable for gathering.

The cliff dwellers were skilled weavers and potters. Samples of their painted bowls, tools and weapons can be viewed at the ranger station by the footbridge along the Gila River and at the Gila Visitor Center, just three miles away.

Although the cliff dwellings are a popular spot, with a dozen or more visitors sometimes climbing in and out of the different rooms, voices are invariably hushed in the caves. The acoustics of the caves and respect for a mysterious past invite quiet conversation and more thought than talk.

Past the dwellings, the trail leads along the face of the cliff, gradually down to the canyon and back to the footbridge, completing the circle but always leaving the question: Why did they disappear?

Archaeologists can offer only sketchy theories as to why the cliff dwellers vanished or where they went. Drought, disease or tribal wars are possible explanations. Some think the cliff dwellers drifted south into Mexico, where they merged with other Pueblo cultures. Others think they just died off.

A pueblo site adjacent to the cliff dwellings, the so-called TJ site, may also be visited. This tour is by appointment only.

Campgrounds near the Gila Cliff Dwellings offer rest rooms and drinking water. A general store and gas station are nearby at Gila Hot Springs, while restaurant and motel accommodations are available in Silver City.

Gila Cliff Dwellings National Monument is open from 8 a.m. to 6 p.m. Memorial Day weekend through Labor Day weekend and 9 a.m. to 4 p.m. the rest of the year. For information, call the Gila Visitor Center at (505) 536-9461 or Gila National Forest headquarters at (505) 388-8201.

Next page—Without obvious modern conveniences such as stairs, escalators and elevators, the Mogollón Indians managed to scale steep precipices on a regular basis to endure daily life. Photo by Mark Nohl.

Charles Stallings

Selenite crystals fan out in a rim around the periphery of Lake Lucero.

Lake Lucero Tour

> *As the climate shifted from cold and wet to warm and dry, the lake evaporated and the crystals grew.*

by Dianne deLeon-Stallings

More than 30,000 years ago, a vast lake covered the land at the eastern foothills of the San Andres Mountains, a rib of peaks that separates Las Cruces from the Tularosa Basin in south-central New Mexico.

Long since dried by sun and sparse rainfall, Lake Lucero still provides an integral step in the 200-million year process that created and continues to replenish the 230-square-mile sea of white gypsum dunes that constitutes White Sands National Monument.

The opportunity to view the lake comes only once each month when the National Park Service conducts a car caravan tour. The lake lies in the southwestern corner of the national monument, accessible only by crossing a 15-mile section of the White Sands Missile Range.

Although the lake is billed as the source of the white sand, in truth,

the San Andres provide gypsum, the raw material. The lake acts as a processing plant.

Approaching Lake Lucero from the south, the sun seems to shimmer off a sprawling expanse of water captured in two depressions connected by a thin canal. But as the caravan nears the entrance to the lake, the illusion evaporates, leaving behind only selenite crystals to reflect the sun's rays.

Before starting the three-quarter-mile hike to the lake bed, a park ranger stresses that the process in the basin occurs nowhere else in the world.

"Gypsum is different from all other materials," Ranger John Mangimeli explains. "While it takes eons for other rocks to break down, gypsum is soluble and will dissolve in rain or snow."

Dunes have not formed on the west side of the San Andres be-

143

Above—A dry, twisting piece of wood indicates the fate of most organisms making a living on the lake bed of Lake Lucero.

cause gypsum there is washed into the Río Grande, he says.

"But no river runs out of here," Mangimeli says. "Every drop stays here and runs to the lowest point it finds. That's Lake Lucero [at 3,887 feet above sea level]. Then it just sits there as the water evaporates, leaving the gypsum behind."

The crusty, 20-square-mile lake bottom is dry most of the year. "Usually, there are just a few pools a few inches deep after a heavy rain," Mangimeli says. Sometimes water is visible in the lake because the underground water table is high, fed by runoff from the Sacramento Mountains to the east.

The deep gullies leading to the lake testify to the days of former glory for Lake Lucero. The gully bottoms are littered with iciclelike selenite crystals as long as 18 inches and brown from impurities.

The crystals grow in layered plates at the lake bed's outer edge, but as they are tumbled by the wind and beaten by the rain, they break down into flakes. By the time they reach the dunes, along with minute gypsum fragments, they turn into grains of pure white sand.

The geological process behind the dunes' formation began during the Permian Period when an ancient sea extended into southeastern New Mexico. As it retreated, deposits of calcium sulphate gypsum were left in small lagoons and bays. Gypsum separated from the saltwater by evaporation, creating a gypsum strata as thick as 650 feet. Seventy million years ago, the formation uplifted, but 60 million years later, faults developed and a section 100 miles long and 30 miles wide collapsed, forming the Tularosa Basin.

Cliffs on both sides of the basin

contained deposits of gypsum, limestone and shale. Unprotected from the erosive effects of wind and rain, the minerals washed from the cliff faces into the waters of a prehistoric lake that dominated the basin 30,000 years ago. As the climate shifted from cold and wet to warm and dry, the lake evaporated and the crystals grew.

Still, the dunes might never have formed if a prevalent southwesterly wind pattern had not developed about the same time, separating, breaking down and carrying the fragments.

Visitors can view the ruins of the 1897 homestead of José and Felipe Lucero, whose ranch at one time encompassed 20,000 acres. Today the landscape consists of mesquite, creosote and tumbleweeds.

The entrance to the missile range is between mile markers 174-175 on U.S. 70 south of Alamogordo.

Plan on a four-hour trip south from Albuquerque by way of Interstate 25, east on U.S. 380 to Carrizozo and south on U.S. 54 to Alamogordo.

Bring something to drink and comfortable walking shoes. Visitors are allowed about an hour to explore the lake bed. The entire tour takes about three hours.

Contact the White Sands visitor center about monthly tours at (505) 479-6124.

Above—*The dry, crystalized lake bed of Lake Lucero presents a sharp contrast to the surrounding countryside. A prehistoric lake dominated the area 30,000 years ago.*

A Southwestern botanical garden, featuring many varieties of cactus, adds to the serene beauty of Pancho Villa State Park in Columbus, near the Mexican border.

Pancho Villa State Park

A conspiracy theory even holds that America provoked Villa to give its troops combat experience in preparation for World War I.

by Jon Bowman

A pockmarked knoll of blood-red basalt towers over the cacti and thorny desert bushes of Pancho Villa State Park.

The volcanic outcropping, known as Villa Hill, makes a perfect symbol for a park commemorating the last armed invasion of the continental United States.

Mexican guerrilla fighters led by the charismatic Gen. Francisco "Pancho" Villa struck the isolated border town of Columbus, under the cover of a moonless night, on March 9, 1916. In the fierce melee that followed, about 20 Americans and at least 100 Villistas died before the general called off his assault and vanished back into his mountain hideaways in Chihuahua.

Historians still debate why the raid occurred. Revenge is the most commonly cited cause. Villa had maintained close relations with many Americans, even going hunting with U.S. Gen. John "Black Jack" Pershing, who later led the unsuccessful expedition into Mexico to find and punish Villa.

But the revolutionary leader felt betrayed when the United States threw its support behind one of his rivals, Venustiano Carranza. Many see the Columbus raid as a clear-cut case of retaliation.

Others, however, have advanced more elaborate theories to explain the attack. Some argue that Villa and his horsemen stormed into Columbus to seize supplies they paid for, but had not received. Some say an aggressive newsreel company instigated the raid as a brazen publicity stunt. A conspiracy theory even holds that America provoked Villa to give its troops combat experience in preparation for World War I.

The 15,000 soldiers pressed into

Mark Nohl

action for Pershing's campaign did usher in a new era of warfare. For the first time in military history, they used biplanes for aerial surveillance, as well as gas-powered cars, motorcycles and trucks.

To this day, controversy sparked by the raid continues. As Pancho Villa State Park ranger Carlos Gamboa says, "Some people think the park should be renamed after Pershing. They think Pancho Villa was a bad influence. But let's face it, he's the man who put Columbus on the map."

Historic photos and relics from the time of the raid can be seen today in the park headquarters, the old Columbus customs house built in 1902. The park contains a few other remnants of Camp Furlong, the Army base that Villa's forces overran and torched.

But these aging structures aren't the main calling cards for Pancho Villa State Park. That distinction belongs to its extensive Southwest botanical gardens, which provide a serene backdrop for reflecting on a bloody chapter in history.

Spearlike yuccas and agaves, squat barrel cacti, bright purple chollas, flowering ocotillos and lowly mesquite and creosote bushes cover the 49-acre grounds. Stone-lined paths crisscross through this prickly maze, leading up to Villa Hill, where both the American and Mexican flags fly.

The promontory offers excellent views of the many mountain ranges that flank Columbus. These include the stark Tres Hermanas (Three Sisters) Peaks and the Florida Mountains, site of another state park, Rock Hound, where visitors can haul off geodes and fascinating gemstones.

To reach Pancho Villa State Park, exit from Interstate 10 in Deming and travel 35 miles south on N.M. 11. Look out for fleet-footed road-runners, a common sight tooling along highways in the area.

Winter is a good time of year to visit. Snows are infrequent and usually light. Daytime temperatures can top 100 degrees Fahrenheit in summer, but seldom drop below freezing even in January.

Pancho Villa State Park, (505) 531-2711, is equipped with rest rooms, showers, picnic shelters and spaces for overnight camping. A motel and RV park also exist in Columbus.

For an authentic taste of Mexico, cross the border into Las Palomas, a thriving community with shops and cantinas. ❖

Above—A ramada at Pancho Villa State Park gives refuge from sunlight. **Next page**—*A towering century plant colors the grounds at the state park.* Photo by Mark Nohl.

CENTRAL

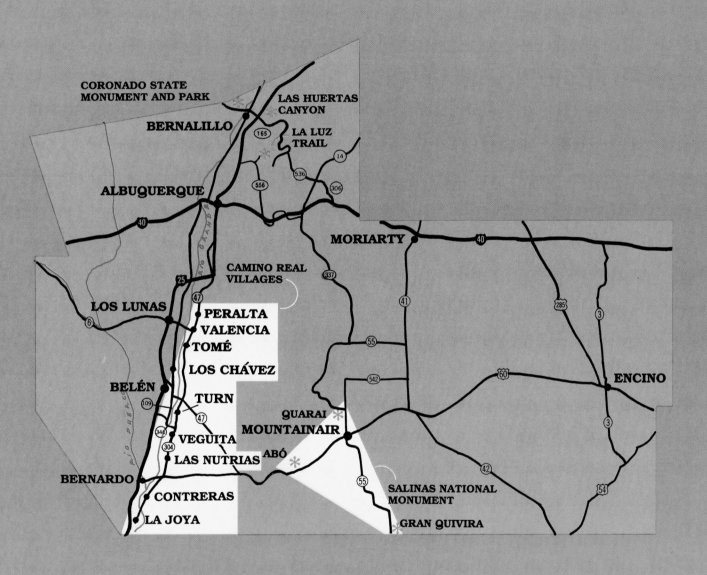

CORONADO STATE
MONUMENT AND PARK

LAS HUERTAS
CANYON

BERNALILLO

165

LA LUZ
TRAIL

14

536

ALBUQUERQUE

556

306

40

MORIARTY

40

CAMINO REAL
VILLAGES

337

25

285

47

LOS LUNAS

41

3

6

PERALTA

VALENCIA

TOMÉ

55

LOS CHÁVEZ

542

60

ENCINO

BELÉN

TURN

109

47

QUARAI

3

346

MOUNTAINAIR

VEGUITA

304

ABÓ

42

LAS NUTRIAS

BERNARDO

55

54

CONTRERAS

SALINAS NATIONAL
MONUMENT

LA JOYA

GRAN QUIVIRA

Mark Nohl

The newly improved Veterans Memorial park in Jarales.

Camino Real Villages

The drive is a kaleidoscope of ancient adobe houses, amid the backdrop of a brilliant turquoise sky.

by Kathleen Raphael

As the interstates cross the state carrying visitors quickly from one town to the next, it is easy to forget the deliberate and hard-won steps of the early trailblazers who left an indelible legacy in New Mexico. One of the earliest and most important trails was *El Camino Real* or the royal road.

First used in the 1500s by Spanish explorers, it stretched from Mexico City to Santa Fe. Running along the Río Grande from present-day El Paso, it headed through the Jornada del Muerto (Journey of Death) in the southern part of the state. As expeditions trekked north, they crisscrossed the Río Grande, establishing settlements east and west of the river.

For the traveler with time and an interest in the past, some of these timeless villages along the *Camino Real* can be seen on the back roads.

Heading south from Albuquerque, take the N.M. 47 exit to Peralta, a community of about 500 people. Old-timers here still remember when spring meant the alfalfa fields along the road began to turn green. Today, the community offers service stations and eateries along the four-lane, undivided highway.

South of Peralta at the Valencia Y, N.M. 47 narrows to two lanes, the roadside conveniences thin out and a more rural setting abounds.

Along this road on Good Friday, the faithful make pilgrimages to the crosses atop Tomé Hill. This farming community was named for Tomé Domínguez de Mendoza, one of Gov. Antonio de Otermín's men, who built a home near the hill before the 1680 Pueblo Revolt. Domínguez never returned after the revolt, but the village still bears his name.

Five miles south, near Belén, the road forks. N.M. 47 heads toward Mountainair and N.M. 304 winds around several small communities. Casa Colorado, Veguita, Las Nutrias—the names of these villages reflect their Spanish heritage. The drive is a kaleidoscope of ancient adobe houses, amid the backdrop of a brilliant turquoise sky. Looking to the west, the craggy peaks of Las Ladrones, or thieves' mountains, hug the horizon. Closer in, pale bluffs run along the Río Grande, crowning the dappled clusters of cottonwoods that bend and twist along the edge of the river.

Following N.M. 304 south, the road junctions with U.S. 60. To the west is Bernardo, site of a store and gas station.

Staying south on N.M. 304, the road passes the small village of Contreras, then three miles later,

follows an incline to La Joya in the river basin.

A Piro Indian pueblo once was located at the present site of La Joya. Known as Sevilleta, it was abandoned after the Pueblo Revolt. Recolonized in the 1800s, the name was changed to La Joya de Sevilleta and today it is called La Joya, meaning jewel in Spanish.

The town, with its red-walled adobes, is literally the end of the road. From here, the traveler must return north along N.M. 304, cross U.S. 60 and backtrack north.

At Casa Colorado (called Turn on the state map), N.M. 304 junctions with N.M. 346. Heading west on N.M. 346, crossing the Río Grande and then heading north, N.M. 109 passes Jarales. (Please note that N.M. 346 and 109 are not listed on the state highway map.)

Jarales, which means thickets, is west of the Río Grande and just

Above—*This pastoral setting in the small village of Tomé seems isolated today, but it once saw plenty of traffic in earlier times by being situated close to El Camino Real, which for centuries was the only link between Santa Fe and Mexico.*

south of Belén. The village is home of a T-33 jet fighter that is part of the Veterans Memorial next to the Senior Citizens Center. A monument in the park lists names of area veterans.

Heading north, the P & M Farm Museum overflows with farm memorabilia. After years of collecting, the rooms are filled with antiques. Outside, Model Ts, a horse-drawn hearse, a stagecoach and many other antique vehicles are on display.

Crossing the railroad tracks and north a few miles is Belén. From here, the traveler can choose a speedy trip home on Interstate 25 or head north on N.M. 47.

The round-trip from Peralta is about 80 miles. The amount of time it takes is up to the traveler, depending on stops and side trips.

Each mile shares something unique with the visitor. Teacup vil-

lages and the wide-open spaces of glorious Southwestern landscapes make these roads well worth taking. ❖

Above—Early New Mexico settlers relied heavily on their religious convictions. Here, Our Lady of Guadalupe stands strong in the small village of Peralta along the route of El Camino Real.

Visitors are treated to a spectacular view, as well as an opportunity to tour a reconstructed kiva.

Coronado State Monument and Park

Pottery and stone objects survived the centuries, but time took a greater toll on the perishable aspects of life. . . .

by Mark Utgaard

A spectacular view of the Sandía Mountains greets visitors at Coronado State Monument and Park outside Bernalillo.

People from around the world come to the monument on the western bank of the Río Grande to see its 15th-century Pueblo art.

But it's the view, unobstructed by the works of man, that keeps visitors lingering.

"It's a tremendous view of the river, the bosque and the Sandías beyond," says Terese Ulivarri, a state parks regional manager.

The featured Pueblo art was discovered during the excavation of the pueblo ruins of Kuaua before 1940. In that year, the monument was dedicated in commemoration of the 400th anniversary of the exploration of New Mexico by Francisco Vázquez de Coronado.

Coronado and his army of 1,200 arrived in New Mexico in 1540 and by autumn, following rumors of golden cities, came to the Río Grande Valley.

"This Nuestra Señora river [Río Grande] flows through a broad valley planted with fields of maize. There are cottonwood groves. There are 12 pueblos," wrote Hernando de Alvarado, one of Coronado's companions.

The Spanish called the valley the Province of Tiguex and at Coronado State Monument are the ruins of the northernmost of the 12 pueblos. The nearby Sandía Pueblo people call it *kuaua*, meaning "evergreen" in their Tiwa language.

Contrary to conventional belief, it is unlikely Coronado wintered at Kuaua in 1540 through 1542. Monument Manager Nathan Stone says few Spanish artifacts were found during excavation.

"There is not a lot of evidence of

Above—*Yuccas, cacti and other native plants color the front of the museum at Coronado State Monument, a classic Pueblo Revival building by John Gaw Meem.*

Coronado being here except possible crossbow points," Stone says. "They found more evidence at Puaray."

Puaray is another Tiguex ruin a mile south of Kuaua where a 1985 excavation unearthed 16th-century Spanish nails, clothing hooks and metal plates.

Yet Coronado probably visited Kuaua and walked its bustling plazas and passed what, four centuries later, would become a spectacular archaeological find.

During the 1930s excavation of Kuaua, scientists were stunned to find a kiva frescoed with images of Kuaua's gods and the gifts of the gods to the people.

"The kiva mural is like a photo album of the people," Stone says.

Pottery and stone objects survived the centuries, but time took a greater toll on the perishable aspects of life at Kuaua, Stone says.

"The mural shows us clothing styles and three different hairstyles. I like the detail in the corn maiden's hair buns, tied with beads. The jewelry, earrings and weaving designs all put you more in touch with them as people.

"And there is a very tight theme in all the paintings: rain and water. It comes from clouds, the mouths of birds, fish and pots.

"Being farmers, this makes sense. They had water on their minds quite a bit," he says.

At the center of the monument is the museum, a striking New Mexico-style building designed by John Gaw Meem. The visitor can see a collection of 15 panels taken from the kiva for study and preservation.

Each panel, faded and sometimes difficult to visualize, is accompanied by a reproduction with narration of its meaning.

A trail beginning at the museum takes visitors through the ruins of Kuaua, its walls partially reconstructed. At its greatest occupation, Kuaua had 1,200 ground-level rooms and rose 3 stories.

The trail leads to a reconstructed kiva where the visitor can climb down for a feel of how the kiva art might have appeared at the time of its creation.

A second trail winds down from the ruins to the edge of the Río Grande. Under rustic cedar ramadas is the view Ulivarri praised.

The sound of the river flowing past mixes with the wind. Across the river birds chatter in the bosque. Beyond this river forest the Sandías rise into the blue.

A quarter-mile from the monument is Coronado State Park. It has 31 camping sites on a low bluff above the river.

The park and monument are lo-cated on N.M. 44 one mile west of Bernalillo.

The park is well-used but sel-dom full, Ulivarri says.

The monument is open daily and admission is charged to everyone more than 15 years old. For more information, call (505) 867-5351.

The park is also open daily and fees are charged for camping, with or without electricity, and picnick-ing. For more information call (505) 867-5589.

Above—From shelters along the Río Grande at Coronado State Monument, campers and picnickers can ponder the times when conquistadores first encountered Pueblo Indians in the New World.

Toby Jurovics

Granite spires and craggy buttresses flank La Luz Trail as it winds to the top of Sandía Peak.

La Luz Trail

> *... climbing La Luz is the botanical equivalent of a trek from the Sonoran Desert of Mexico to the forests of British Columbia.*

by Mark L. Taylor

In Spanish it means "The Light," but in any language and from any angle, La Luz Trail is a magical journey of time and space.

From the cholla cactus of the Sandía Mountains foothills to the towering pines and tiny alpine flowers of the ragged limestone crest, climbing La Luz is the botanical equivalent of a trek from the Sonoran Desert of Mexico to the forests of British Columbia.

In one of his most famous essays, conservationist and onetime New Mexico resident Aldo Leopold urged readers to "think like a mountain." An interesting perspective to ponder as with every step up La Luz, the hazy sprawl of Albuquerque gives way to desert-clean expanses beyond the city, to Mount Taylor and the Zuñi Mountains.

La Luz is the best maintained and most used of three trails that scale the massive granite and limestone flanks of the Sandías' western face. The other two, Embudito and the newly opened Pino trails, are to the south. While those trails also offer wonderful scenery, there is something especially exhilarating about the passage on La Luz.

Total hiking distance from the trailhead parking lot at the Juan Tabo picnic area to the upper tram terminal is 7.8 miles. The elevation gain is a lung-sucking 3,700 feet. The well-marked trail is easy to follow, yet the challenge is enough to make a tenderfoot feel like Sir Edmund Hillary.

The trailhead is reached by driving north on Tramway Boulevard from Interstate 40, or go east on Tramway from Interstate 25. Go north on the Juan Tabo turnoff and follow the road into the foothills. Turn right between the second set

Right—*Towering cliffs on the western face of the Sandía Mountains give hikers on La Luz Trail exhilarating highs.*

of stone columns and continue past the picnic area to an upper-level parking lot at the end of the road. A U.S. Forest Service sign on the south side of the parking area marks the beginning of the trail.

The first section of the trail follows a series of switchbacks, whose monotony is compensated for by an expanding view of the Río Grande Valley.

At the one-mile point, be sure not to wander off on the Tramway Trail junction. Soon after this point the small piñon and juniper trees are slowly replaced by larger trees,

such as ponderosa pine, and the forest grows taller.

After crossing a small seep, you will enter Chimney Canyon, and after that the stomach-dropping scenery of upper La Cueva Canyon. Take the time here to hike—carefully—on some of the small side paths to get the full impact of the soaring granite spires, buttresses and vertical drops. Lie on your stomach and watch the birds soar beneath you.

After this point, the trail switchbacks up a talus slope of car-sized boulders and broken trees. Some

feel this is the most strenuous section of the trail, but the beauty is more likely to take your breath away than the hike.

The trail then passes through a small saddle where it branches into two possible paths. The left-hand path follows a short, steep scramble to the gift shop on top of the crest. The south trail follows a moderate grade along the limestone band of the crest and ends a few yards from the patio of the High Finance Restaurant.

A strong hiker can make the climb in about three hours. The

Above—Warm and spirit-building sunsets from atop Sandía Peak are as reliable as the blue New Mexico sky.

rest of us should figure on four to five hours. You might come across some crazed characters who actually run up La Luz, but that's another story.

A word of warning. Despite closeness to the city, La Luz Trail traverses an officially designated federal wilderness area. This is rough country and hikers should wear sturdy hiking boots and carry plenty of water, food, matches, flashlight and bad-weather gear. Every year, people manage to wander off the well-marked trail and become lost. Some are hurt—even killed—in falls.

Mountain bicycles are not al-

Toby Jurovics

lowed and dogs should be leashed if you really think the dog should not be left at home.

Enjoy the serenity and special light of La Luz. Leave your preconceptions behind and open up some special room in your heart for this most unique of New Mexico hikes.

For more information on hiking La Luz Trail or any of the other wonderful Sandía Mountain hikes, refer to Mike Hill's *Hikers and Climbers Guide to the Sandías*. The book is published by the University of New Mexico Press and comes with a dandy hiking map.

Mark Nohl

Many wonders lie hidden within Las Huertas Canyon near Albuquerque.

Las Huertas Canyon

by Dan Scurlock

At the north end of the Sandía Mountains, less than an hour's drive from Albuquerque, is Las Huertas (large gardens) Canyon. Here travelers can view or explore four biological zones, towering cliffs of pink granite or gray limestone, and Sandía Man Cave, where some of New Mexico's earliest residents lived.

The canyon was named by early Spaniards who came in search of precious metals found in veins among the granite outcrops. Some silver, copper and lead was mined from the 1600s to the early 1800s and area residents still talk about the fabled Montezuma Mine located somewhere along the lower part of the canyon. Here, the local story goes, a rich deposit of silver lies sealed by rocks and dirt thrown into the mouth of the mine by Pueblo Indians during their revolt against the Spaniards in 1680.

Following the settlement of the Las Huertas land grant in 1768, Spanish hunters, woodcutters and goatherds frequented the canyon. Later, a few Anglo miners and homesteaders tried to eke out a living, but almost all failed. Most of the canyon became public land in 1906 when the Manzano National Forest Reserve, forerunner of Cíbola National Forest, was created. In the 1920s, N.M. 165 was constructed through the canyon.

The canyon has been shaped over millions of years by runoff, some of which ends up in the crystal-clear waters of Las Huertas Creek. This stream, which begins at nearly 10,000 feet, cascades down the floor of the canyon past the old, land-grant village of Placitas more than 4,000 feet below.

As you drive southward through Placitas and enter the lower canyon, a dense, piñon-juni-

160

per forest blankets the slopes, while New Mexico locust, box elder and other water-loving trees and shrubs crowd the banks of Las Huertas Creek.

About three miles up the canyon, you'll see the parking area for Sandía Man Cave. From here, a steep, half-mile foot trail leads to the limestone cave, a national historic site. This designation followed spectacular finds made by University of New Mexico archaeologists more than 50 years ago.

In the lower levels of the cave they found the distinctive stone tools and weapons of people who lived in the canyon more than 10,000 years ago. With these artifacts were the bones of several animals, some of them extinct—a horse, camel, mammoth, mastodon and a giant bison—that the Sandía people hunted among the cold, moist forests and meadows that existed at the end of the last ice age.

As you continue south up the canyon and along the road, the turnoff to the Las Huertas picnic area comes into view. Here, scattered along the creek, are picnic tables, grills and rest rooms maintained by the U.S. Forest Service. Footpaths lead up the creek through towering white fir trees and, in summer or fall, carpets of colorful wildflowers.

The historic Cooper-Ellis Ranch spreads out about three-quarters of a mile beyond the picnic area. The Ellis family came to New Mexico in the late 1880s and built a 2-story, log cabin on a homestead along the banks of Las Huertas Creek. Acquired by the Coopers in the early part of the century, the property has been maintained by the family and the 100-year-old cabin is on the State Registry of

Above—Archaeologists unearthed a wealth of evidence linked to the existence of prehistoric man at Sandía Man Cave in Las Huertas Canyon. The find dates early humans at the cave more than 10,000 years ago.

Above—A steep but scenic foot trail leads to the Sandía Man Cave, where stone tools and weapons of early man were found along with bones of several different types of animals, some of them extinct.

Historic Landmarks.

After a mile or so of turns, N.M. 165 intersects N.M. 536, a paved highway leading to Sandía Crest or to N.M. 14.

For the serious hiker, the 10-K trail, which begins on N.M. 536, skirts the head of Las Huertas Creek, affording spectacular views of the canyon. Late spring, summer and early fall are the most enjoyable times for hiking. Extended snowfalls reaching depths of a foot or more necessitate closing the road during the winter.

Flowers and trees, as well as the animals who live in the canyon, are part of the 38,000-acre Sandía Mountain Wilderness Area. Among the larger animals within the wilderness, but rarely seen, are black bear and mountain lion and the more-common mule deer. A lucky visitor might see a golden eagle or find a paw print of a bear or lion along the creek. Probably the most common and showiest of all the creatures are the butterflies. Attracted by the moist conditions and many wildflowers, everything from tiny hairstreaks to large swallowtails can be found at Las Huertas throughout the summer.

There are two ways to reach Las Huertas Canyon via N.M. 165. One is to exit east from Interstate 25 at Bernalillo, through Placitas to the lower canyon. To access the south canyon, turn west off N.M. 14 at San Antonito onto N.M. 536 and drive 7.5 miles to the junction of N.M. 165 near the Balsam Glade picnic area. Additional information may be obtained from U.S. Forest Service offices at nearby Tijeras or in Albuquerque. ✺

Located in the eastern foothills of the Manzano Mountains, the Quarai ruin is one of three related sites at the Salinas National Monument in central New Mexico.

Salinas National Monument

> *Salt, hauled all the way to Chihuahua for silver-ore processing in the great mines, was the Spaniards' primary interest in the area.*

by Michael Richie

The view from the 6,650-foot-high Gran Quivira Ruins at Salinas National Monument takes in a 360-degree panorama of rolling, piñon-juniper forested meadows, where the mountains east of the Río Grande Valley drop gradually down to the Great Plains.

At its height in the 1500s before the Spaniards arrived, Cueloze, as the inhabitants called it, was a thriving outpost for the Anasazi world. Numerous building complexes contained up to 3,000 rooms, which sheltered as many people, making it one of the largest pueblos in the Southwest. Surrounding meadows were terraced and irrigated via elaborate water-catchment systems. Maize, squash, melons, beans and cotton flourished.

Cueloze commanded a unique trading position on the Anasazi frontier. Influenced by Plains Indians and by the Apache, the local diet was rich in buffalo meat. These people were taller, more robust than the average Anasazi. Salt from dried lake-bed deposits gave them a trade specialty. Unearthed parrot feathers, copper bells and mother-of-pearl jewelry show that the pueblo was part of an economic network stretching from the Mississippi to the Pacific, from southern Colorado to Central America.

Cueloze had a unique role as a melting pot for pre-Columbian cultures of the region. Continuous habitation in the Estancia Valley goes back more than 10,000 years when Paleo-Indians hunted elephants in nearby swamps. As the land slowly dried, a hunter/gatherer culture moved into the area from the Río Grande Valley. Population concentration accompanied increased agriculture. The most

Right—The evening sunlight casts mystical shadows upon the wondrous stone walls at Quarai, one of many ancient Pueblo settlements where Spanish conquistadores and missionaries left their influence. **Opposite**—*Superior building skills are evident at the aging walls in Gran Quivira. Pursuing rumors, Francisco Vázquez de Coronado searched to no avail to find a "Gran Quivira," a village purported to be made out of gold.*

lasting influence came in the 1100s from the sophisticated Chacoan Anasazi peoples to the northwest. Multistoried pueblos, water-control systems and elaborate kachina rituals in underground, circular kivas had completely transformed the previous culture by the 1300s. With the exception of a mass migration from the Zuñi area in the 1550s, Cueloze enjoyed a stable, prosperous existence on the Anasazi frontier until the 1620s.

Ironically, the brief, unsuccessful Spanish occupation left the most imposing reminder. The San Buenaventura Mission ruins tower 50 feet over surrounding pueblo walls. Huge by Indian standards, the church measured 140 feet long by 70 feet wide, with 6-foot-thick walls, ornamentally carved, massive ceiling beams supporting herring-boned cross members, and an altar room built 8 feet above ground level. Constructed in 1660, the mission was abandoned less than 20 years later in the face of Apache raids and drought. The Spaniards and Indians left Cueloze for the Río Grande Valley in despair.

Gran Quivira is one of the three related sites centered around Mountainair and now included in Salinas Missions National Monument. Quarai ruin lies eight miles north of Mountainair on N.M. 55, Abó is nine miles west on U.S. 60 and Gran Quivira 25 miles south on N.M. 55. An additional visitor's center at the historic Schaffer Hotel in Mountainair gives an overview of all three sites.

The rationale for grouping these three pueblos into one national monument depends on the presence of missions at each. They formed the core of a nine-pueblo-strong region the Spanish called their "Salinas Province." Salt, hauled all the way to Chihuahua for silver-ore processing in the great mines, was the Spaniards' primary interest in the area.

Although the churches were all constructed from the same general plan, each mission site has a unique character. Located at a lush, spring-fed, cottonwood-shaded meadow in the foothills of the Manzano Mountains, the Quarai mission epitomizes the strength of convictions that sus-

tained Franciscan fathers in New Mexico. La Purisma Concepcíon de Cuarac church was part of a huge, fortresslike compound containing priest and staff quarters, storerooms, an inner plaza and garden with small orchard, stables, even a watchtower or *torreón*. Built in 1630 and abandoned in 1670, like the other Salinas missions it wasn't in use for long.

A nearby, perennially running stream and location right on the salt route to the Río Grande gave Abó its particular character.

Spanish influence eventually came to dominate the Pueblo world. But on the Salinas Province frontier it was short-lived. This thriving region supported a pre-Columbian population of 10,000. Anasazi success came from adaptation to and harmony with a harsh environment. A melancholy hint suffuses these ruins. The wind's refrain across crumbling pueblo walls sings a song worth remembering. ❖